PATRICIA RAILING
Editor

Essays on

VICTORY OVER THE SUN

Artists . Bookworks 2009

Published in England by
Artists . Bookworks
28 Freshfield Bank
Forest Row, East Sussex
RH18 5GH

This is Volume 2 (ISBN 978 0 946311 18 7)
sold only as part of a two-volume Set:
ISBN 978 0 946311 19 4

This two volume set has been made possible by the generosity of

Artists Books and Writings, Inc.

Printed in Belgium by
Die Keure nv
Kleine Pathoekeweg 3
8000 Brugge

CONTENTS

5   Publisher's Foreword

7   The Creators

8   The Contributors

9   A Note On Russian Futurism

12   The Artists' Society "Union of Youth"

THE THEATRE, THE OPERA   15

17   Anthony Parton
        Killing the Moonlight & Conquering the Sun:
            The Theatrical Origins of Russian Futurist Theatre

31   Nina Gourianova
        Aleksei Kruchenykh's Theatre of Alogism

THE WORD   45

47   Aleksei Kruchenykh
        New Ways of the Word (1913)

57   Christopher Dempsey
        On *Zaum* and its Use in *Victory Over the Sun*

ENTER THE PERFORMANCE   67

69   Caroline Wallis and Patricia Railing
        Journey in Space-Time in the Vehicle of Destiny

THE SETS & COSTUMES   83

85   John Milner
        Malevich's *Victory Over the Sun*

THE MUSIC   99

101   Christopher Dempsey
        A Musical Assessment of *Victory Over the Sun*

THE LEGACY   117

119   John Milner
        'All is well that begins well and has no end'
            The After-Life of *Victory Over the Sun*

128   Bibliography

137   Index to Volumes 1 and 2

Publisher's Foreword

This is the second volume of the set devoted to *Victory Over the Sun*.

It contains scholarly essays that bring light to various aspects of theatre in Russia at the time, and to the many ideas that inspired the creation of the opera in language, set and costume design, and music.

Authors from several disciplines and different countries were invited to contribute, making the volume something of a kaleidoscope of colours, styles, and approaches to their subject. This was encouraged and, indeed, is considered an asset in a project where the creators – and Kruchenykh even made the point – bring the new in many ways, each with his or her own kind of consciousness.

Kruchenykh himself makes a guest appearance in this volume. As a master of the creative word, he is certainly the best person to explain the reasons and methods that underlie his transrational writing, revealing his own kind of consciousness. His article, 'New Ways of the Word', was written at the time he wrote *Victory Over the Sun* and it appeared in a volume of poetry and theory, *The Three*, in September 1913. It is included here in a new translation by Christiana Bryan and S. I. Tverdoklebov.

The performance of *Victory Over the Sun* in 1913 is famous and familiar to literature, painting, music, and theatre, but this is the first time in English that it is drawn together as a whole. In this collection of articles on *Victory Over the Sun*, the different arts meet in a new dialogue.

The publishers express their warmest thanks to Nina Gourianova and Elizabeth Phillips, as well as to Caroline Wallis and Melvyn Wallis, for all their good offices, and to Ilya Zilberberg for always being there.

And, of course, for the good offices of Artists Books and Writings, Inc. Their sponsorship of *Victory Over the Sun* is an acknowledgement of its importance and a gift to scholars of several artistic disciplines, and to all those who like books that reveal the New.

Patricia Railing, Director
Artists . Bookworks

THE CREATORS

VIKTOR/VELIMIR KHLEBNIKOV (1885 – 1922) was born in Astrakhan of thoroughly Slavic descent. Mathematician, ornithologist and wordsmith, Khlebnikov investigated how the word and number reveal human history and events in time – he was called the King of Time by his friends, and Chairman of the Globe by himself. His Prologue for *Victory Over the Sun* is made up almost entirely of neologisms, or what he called 'sound-writing,' *zvukopis*, based on old Slavonic roots.

ALEKSEI KRUCHENYKH (1886 – 1969) studied graphic art in Odessa. Moving to Moscow, then St. Petersburg, he published over 30 illustrated books of poetry together with his poet and painter friends. His libretto for *Victory Over the Sun* reflects their common interest in Parisian Cubism, Cubism of the word. Kruchenykh called this *zaum*, or transrational language, where linear logic is revoked in favour of the irrational, so inspiring creative imagination.

MIKHAIL MATIUSHIN (1861 – 1934) graduated from the Moscow Conservatory in 1881 and played in the Court Orchestra, 1882 – 1913. He studied painting 1886 – 1889 and 1904 – 1908. He was a co-founder of the Artists' Society "Union of Youth" in 1909 and exhibited with it, 1910 – 1914. He published his *Guide to Studying Quarter-tones for Violin* in 1915. His compositions, mainly for piano or violin, are little known and have been little studied.

KAZIMIR MALEVICH (1879 – 1935) studied at art school in Kiev then Moscow, graduating in 1905. His interest in Parisian Cubism and his own Cubist painting led to his collaboration with Aleksei Kruchenykh on *Victory Over the Sun*. Malevich's backdrops for the scenes and the costumes are the visual parallels of the poetic language, both characterised by Cubist fragmentation and shift in time and space.

THE CONTRIBUTORS

CHRISTOPHER DEMPSEY is a musicologist specialising in 20th century Russian/Soviet music. He is currently Curator of the Stearns Collection of Musical Instruments at the University of Michigan, Ann Arbor, Michigan.

NINA GOURIANOVA is a literary and art historian specialising in 20th century Russia. She is author of *Exploring Color – Olga Rozanova and the Early Russian Avant-Garde 1910–1918* (G+B Arts), and *The Literary Writings of Kruchenykh* (Berkeley Slavic Specialities). She is Professor of Russian Studies at Northwestern University, Chicago, Illinois.

JOHN MILNER is an art historian, Professor Emeritus of the University of Newcastle-upon-Tyne, and Professor of Art History, Courtauld Institute, London. His many publications include *Vladimir Tatlin and the Russian Avant-Garde* (Yale University Press), *Kazimir Malevich and the Art of Geometry* (Yale University Press), and *A Dictionary of Russian & Soviet Artists 1420–1970* (Antique Collectors' Club).

ANTHONY PARTON is an art historian and author of *Mikhail Larionov and the Russian Avant-Garde* (Princeton University Press) and of *Natalia Goncharova: The Construction of Russian Modernism 1900–1940* (forthcoming). He is Lecturer in Art History at Durham University, England.

PATRICIA RAILING is an art historian and has published widely on the Russian avant-garde. She is Director of Artists . Bookworks.

EVGENY STEINER is an art historian affiliated with New York University and the Russian Institute for Cultural Research (Moscow). He was Leverhulme Visiting Professor at the University of Manchester, Centre for Eurasian Studies 2006 – 2007. His publications include *Stories for Little Comrades: Revolutionary Artists and the Making of the Early Soviet Children's Books* (University of Washington Press), *Zen-Life: Ikkyu and Beyond* (St. Petersburg: Orientalia) and other books and articles on Russian and Japanese art and culture.

CAROLINE WALLIS is a bio-meteorologist and conducts pioneering research into the effects of solar activity on weather and human health. She is a consultant to a number of international businesses.

A NOTE ON RUSSIAN FUTURISM

There were two Futurisms around 1912: one Italian, the other Russian. And they were not the same.

The Italians placed emphasis on speed, depicting how they saw objects in movement. There are the famous paintings of a hand playing a violin (Balla), a running dog on a leash (Balla), a running man (Boccioni), and a woman dancing (Severini). This quickly led to the focus on speed in the urban and technological environment, so there are paintings of locomotives, automobiles and airplanes. Translated into the art of noises, the urban and technological gave rise to new musical works. In painting, speed and movement were shown using repetitive elements in order to convey how the eye, or the camera, sees movement in space. This device of visual staccato-effects is a kind of Italian logo for their Futurism.

Although there are examples of such a device being used by Russian painters as in canvases depicting a woman sewing on a machine (Udaltsova), a cyclist (Goncharova), or a knifegrinder (Malevich), Futurism in Russia soon became a much more complex phenomenon. It brought together not only what the eye sees as it catches objects in motion, but how the observation shifts when combined with the artist's perception.

This emphasis on perception, which is a mental activity arising out of the stimulation of a visual (or aural or tactile, etc.) sensation, came directly from Parisian Cubism. It is what inspired not only painters such as Malevich – and others like David Burliuk, Natalia Goncharova, and Olga Rozanova, for example – but also poets like Kruchenykh – as well as David Burliuk, again, Khlebnikov, Mayakovsky, and Benedikt Livshits – to engage their own movement in what they depicted (in pigments or in words), whether in the body moving around an object or in the artist's mind moving around in time and across space. It was the artist's own sensations that were the origin of this activity which, transformed into a painting, a poem, or an 'opera', stimulated the spectator's own sensations. This is what the Russians meant by 'Futurism': the inner dynamic movement of our sensations and the resulting perceptions, whether in the creator or the spectator.

So in Russian Futurism, David Burliuk would turn his canvas or sheet of paper around and depict figures from the different points of view, as can be seen on the back cover of the libretto of *Victory Over the Sun*. Here it is not the objects that move but the spectator's sensations and perceptions that move, even in the physical act of turning the image around. This is also what explains the idea that lies behind Malevich's backdrops for *Victory Over the Sun:* he makes the viewer move, imaginatively, in the imagination, as the play progresses. The performance becomes an experience and is experiential – not in the emotions of happy-sad, but by engaging our many sensations-perceptions and setting them in motion.

This same principle led to Kruchenykh's notion of what he called *zaum*, literally, 'beyond mind', usually translated as 'transrational'. In his language creation he started with the sensations of letter-sounds, from which he challenged his mental perceptions and made up new words to convey new meanings as his perceptions shifted. He was challenging linear, literal thinking and learned logical sequences, and opening up possibilities for non-linear, non-literal, non-logical thinking. His writing appears to be non-rational, irrational, and in the better meaning of this word, so it is: it is ir-rational, or not-rational, where 'rational' in this case means 'logical'. Kruchenykh was attacking what we know today as left-brain thinking, and he was appealing to right-brain thinking. It is from this place in the mind, the right brain, that creativity comes, because creativity can only come from seeing connections that the left-brain laws blind us to. Every invention in the world comes from seeing new connections, new relationships.

These are the ideas that permeated painting, poetry and music in Russia from around 1912. And it was called Futurism because these ideas were what would make possible the creation of the new to replace all that was old – outworn, dead, and dying in artistic, social and political structures, together with the lifeless thinking that maintained them in power.

In painting, Russian Futurism was also called 'Cubo-Futurism'. Only days before the performances of *Victory Over the Sun*, Malevich showed a small group of works in the 7th Union of Youth exhibition which he called 'Cubo-Futurist Realism'. These works are thoroughly Cubist in the French manner, but the painter's observations from different points of view became time elements, as aspects of movement. Since time is a concept of the mind, so a mental activity, the Futurist content of these paintings is movement in time. The movement and dynamism are within us, not in the objects, and certainly not on a canvas, which is static. As Malevich wrote in 1915, the Italians discovered only the movement of *things*.

In 1914, Malevich did several works which he classified as 'a-logical'. They are visual parallels to Kruchenykh's transrational poetry. In his paintings, Malevich juxtaposed objects seen with his eyes and in his mind, in memories and in fantasy, from newspaper articles and from his sense of humour.

Necessarily, the notion of 'chaos' is introduced here. Irrational placements of objects or arrangements of words confuse our expectations.

When Malevich and Matiushin say in their interview, published on 1 December 1913 (in Volume 1), that they 'want to turn this world into chaos', they explain this by saying that 'established values are to be broken to pieces' – mainly because they have lost the creative power they once would have had. It is from 'the pieces [that] they want to create new values... opening up new unexpected and invisible relations'. That can only take place in a creative mind, never in a mind restricted to fixed laws of rationality. So, *Victory Over the Sun* introduces 'irrationality', which is a new rationality because it sees connections and relations – invisible ones even, they say.

These 'invisible relations' are time related to space, which is why the librettist so boldly declared, speaking for the Futurists generally, that they wanted to 'masculinise' the world. For in the ancient wisdom which they were drawing on, the masculine *principle* (*not* gender – where physical gender is an *expression* of the principle, not the other way round) represents time, and the feminine *principle* (not gender) represents space. Time had just been discovered in a new way and this was to turn the world upside down and in reverse, a chaos arising in the process of leaving Newton's laws of linear physics and entering Einstein's world of non-linear physics. Here, time offers a new way of being in the world, and a new consciousness.

Khlebnikov, Kruchenykh, Malevich, Matiushin, and their Futurist friends, were truly Men and Women of the Future, and *Victory Over the Sun* shows the process of overturning all that constrains the new from manifesting. After the chaos comes a new order, new organisation, reorganisation.

So they might have said, 'Long live the Future!'

Patricia Railing

NB. This little exposé of what Futurism meant to the creators of *Victory Over the Sun* – and 1913 was the height of Futurism in Russia – was differently explained by art critics. They picked up on only one aspect of the Futurist artists' activities: 'to consciously reject traditions', as one critic put it in 1912. Between 1912 and 1914, the press was full of attacks on the public readings, provocations, lectures, exhibitions and events by the artists of *Victory Over the Sun* and their milieu. So, 'Futurism became a cliché for anything outrageous, incomprehensible, absurd and ludicrous in art life', as Elena Basner concludes. ('Futurism and the Futurists in the Mirror of the Russian Press of the 1910s', *Russian Futurism*, 18).

The word 'Futurism', however, is found now and again after that, used mainly by poets to mean what was 'new'. Even Vasily Kandinsky claimed to be one, declaring in 1921 that 'We are all Futurists'. Then in 1933, Benedikt Livshits gathered up all the innovative artistic initiatives and called them 'Futurism', glorifying an epoch that was now only a memory; recently, several books and exhibitions have been based on his definition. But in late 1913, *Victory Over the Sun* was an encapsulation of all that Russian artists meant by the word 'Futurism'.

THE ARTISTS' SOCIETY "UNION OF YOUTH"

Victory Over the Sun was advertised on posters and in the press as being presented by the Society of Artists "Union of Youth".

The Union of Youth had been founded in late 1909 by a group of painters that included Mikhail Matiushin and his wife, the poetess Elena Guro. In January 1910 a brief statement in the press announced the formation of the group and read:

'"The Union of Youth"

'This is the name for an enterprise of a group of artists that deserves sympathetic attention. Taking into consideration the difficult contemporary situation for artists, especially the artistic youth, due to undoubted over-production, an abundance of exhibitions, the closed nature of societies, the detachment and solitude of artists, all of which make it difficult for new artists to show their skill, the "Union" aims to organise its own centre. This will be something like a museum-club, where links can be established, artists can become acquainted, and where, most importantly, they can get to know each other's work, can listen attentively and freely to arguments and thus new talents can be revealed.

'Here the main aim is not the organisation of exhibitions, which will occur later as a result of the group's essence becoming clear. Rather, it is to allow the possibility of self-examination, free searching, and the elucidation of new paths. What is actually desirable here is a certain crystallisation that is more or less clearly promoted, a new sense of individuality or a new common movement. The idea is new and interesting. As a rule, exhibiting societies and groups are phenomena which are often independent of inner necessity, become burdened by their productivity, and sometimes by a dilettanti character.'

By February 1910 the group had been officially authorised and placed on the register of Petersburg societies.

The founding members begin their statement of Regulations with the sentence:

'The Society of Artists "The Union of Youth" has the aim of familiarising its members with modern trends in art; of developing their aesthetic tastes by means of drawing and painting workshops, as well as discussions on questions of art; and of furthering the mutual rapprochement of people interested in art.'

The group soon had premises, as it was said in the press, 'where twice a week, on Wednesdays and Saturdays, the artists meet, study drawing and discuss their work. Although this circle, which at the moment consists of fifteen artists, has only recently started to function, by means of highly serious communal discussion of their works and the unity of direction, for which they are being organised, it appears that the "union" could come forward and open their exhibition in the first week of Lent. This exhibition will allow the circle to plan its future activities.'

The first exhibition, Union of Youth 1, opened in Petersburg in March 1910, and the last exhibition, Union of Youth 7, opened there in November 1913. During these years it organised public debates on the arts, published three issues of *Union of Youth* in 1912 and 1913, and sponsored musical evenings and theatrical productions, the last being *Victory Over the Sun* and *Vladimir Mayakovsky: A Tragedy*. There had even been the plan to create a museum of modern art, and a few works by Picasso and other Parisian Cubists were purchased for it by one of the members, Voldemar Matvejs (a Latvian who adopted the pseudonym, Vladimir Markov) when he was sent to Paris for this purpose. There was also a great interest in primitive sculpture and Matvejs' books were published by the Union of Youth.

Other painters soon joined, either as members or as guest exhibitors. Among the latter were Natalia Goncharova and Mikhail Larionov, while among the members there were Olga Rozanova, who did the poster advertising *Victory Over the Sun* (in Volume 1), and Kazimir Malevich.

Two of the original members of the Union of Youth included Josif Shkolnik, who painted the sets for Mayakovsky's *Tragedy*, and another painter, Levky Ivanovich Zheverzheev, a wealthy businessman who supplied cloths and other ecclesiastical fittings to the church. Among other events, Zheverzheev became the financier of the two theatrical events of December 1913.

By some strange quirk of fate, the Union of Youth disbanded after the December 1913 performances. Jeremy Howard describes this in his book, *The Union of Youth*, from which these notes and translations of texts have been taken:

'With the publication of [Vladimir] Markov's essays [*Texture, The Art of Easter Island* and *The Reed Pipe*], the Union of Youth, its death toll sounded by *Victory Over the Sun*, ceased to function. Its force, and even *raison d'être*, was spent after the production of the Futurist opera, which can be seen as a statement of the new worldview that the group had encouraged. With the presentation of this worldview, the old order had to be abandoned and, with it, old affiliations and established groups. As if colluding with this, the performance of *Victory Over the Sun* occasioned a dispute in the Union of Youth's ranks that ended with the group being wound up. Zheverzheev, who had personally agreed to subsidise the production, was upset by the scandal it created, especially as the public had been charged very high prices for tickets. He argued with Kruchenykh about payment and refused Matiushin's request to return Malevich's designs. These events led several Union of Youth members to seek official curtailment of the group's collaboration with [the Moscow] Hylaea [group of poets] in a letter to Zheverzheev of 6 December 1913. The chairman responded by refusing to subsidise future ventures, and as a result only the books by Markov, for whom Zheverzheev always seems to have retained respect, were published. Planned exhibitions and the fourth issue of *The Union of Youth* were cancelled. The Union of Youth had served its purpose. It had brought artists together without dogma or preconditions, but its attempts to unify disparate tendencies, at a time of fierce competition for originality, were bound to fail as new allegiances and factions emerged.… . Malevich resigned from the Union of Youth and on 21 February [1914] he wrote to Rozanova referring to the "unfortunate Union".'

Nevertheless, Jeremy Howard continues, 'In 1917 Zheverzheev and Shkolnik tried to resuscitate the Union of Youth' in order to ' "revive the activity of the Society with respect to exhibitions etc.".' Members were to include Malevich and Rozanova as well as many of the new avant-garde artists, but, as Jeremy Howard concludes in the last lines of his book, 'However, only a few meetings were held before the summer, and with the revolutionary events of the autumn the enterprise failed to get off the ground.'

Patricia Railing

Compiled from Jeremy Howard, The Union of Youth. An artists' society of the Russian avant-garde, *Manchester University Press, 1992. Quotations from pages 42, 46, and 223-4.*

THE THEATRE, THE OPERA

'Only those who are in darkness do not see the light – the
deaf do not hear the new sound.'
'The life of a new creation is strong. It is important to see
and hear its appearance in time.'

Mikhail Matiushin, 'Futurism in St. Petersburg:
Performances on the 2nd, 3rd, 4th, and 5th of December 1913',
First Journal of Russian Futurists, January 1914

Anthony Parton

KILLING THE MOONLIGHT
& CONQUERING THE SUN:
THE THEATRICAL ORIGINS OF RUSSIAN FUTURIST THEATRE

Throughout history and across societies a special place has been accorded to the sun, moon and planetary bodies. They have been worshipped and personified and their imagery has filled the literature and art of human culture. In the text of *Genesis*, for example, God sets the sun and the moon in the heavens to establish a natural order for creation and to mark the passage of time.[1] The sun and the moon, therefore, have traditionally been regarded as the inviolable symbols of a natural order that underpins the mechanics of the universe in general and of life on earth in particular.

When the leader of the Italian Futurists, Filippo Marinetti, attempted to 'kill the moonlight' and the Russian avant-garde threatened to 'conquer the sun' they expressed a desire to destroy that established order and to disrupt the passage of time.[2] They set themselves against Nature, against the Church, against established social and political structures and against 'the Fat Man of the Renaissance'. The rhetoric that they employed was a language of rupture. It spoke of anarchy and revolution but it did so in apocalyptic terms. The book of *Revelation*, for example, describes how, at the apocalypse, the sun, moon and heavens will be 'rolled up like a scroll' so that 'there shall be time no longer'.[3] The apocalypse, of which the Futurists dreamed, however, was not divinely ordained but was to be entirely man-made. Futurist rhetoric had no need of religion or God for it spoke of modern man as the architect of his own glorious future.

These are the themes addressed in the Futurist opera *Victory Over the Sun*. The sun is captured and this brings about the end of established order and of sequential time. The capture prepares the way for a new world in which everything is fundamentally altered. There are no sorrows, no mistakes, no affectation and no bending of knees for 'we can imaginatively arrange our belongings as if a rich kingdom were being moved'. (Scene 5) The weak, who are incapable of change and who cannot sustain an existence in this post-revolutionary world, drown themselves, leaving only the Futurian Strongman to take full possession of 'the New Jerusalem' that he has created.

Victory Over the Sun operated in a decisively new and innovative way to challenge received dogmas, to suggest that violent and radical change was both possible and desirable and to point the way to a bright future. The opera was challenging not only at the level of its content, however, but also at the level of its form since it decisively rejected the traditional means of proscenium arch theatre favoured by the bourgeoisie. Conventional narrative is disrupted throughout the opera as one event slides into another. This is a device known as *sdvig* (shift), which was borrowed from the poetical experiments of Aleksei Kruchenykh and Velimir Khlebnikov, and it contributes a Cubist effect to the overall texture of the work. Sometimes there are radical disjunctures in the narrative that remind us of similar techniques employed in Futurist paintings. Conventional speech is likewise disrupted since the libretto is cast in the form of Kruchenykh's and Khlebnikov's transrational poetics known as *zaum*.

The music, too, was challenging since it was scored by Mikhail Matiushin, sometimes using a system of quarter tones. In addition, the sets by Kazimir Malevich were executed in Cubist fashion so as to avoid conventional mimesis. Here Malevich 'collaged' together snatches of images and part words in order to create a pictorial analogue to the inventive transrational libretto. Malevich also employed an unconventional use of stage lighting. According to Benedikt Livshits 'there was just no comparison with the "fairy-light effects" usually employed on the stages of those days', for Malevich used 'blades of light' to dissect the theatrical action at each and every point.[4] This innovative approach to the visual aspects of the opera was even carried into the costumes. In both form and in content, then, *Victory Over the Sun* presented a complex metaphor of revolution. How, then, was such a radical form of theatre possible in 1913?

Folk Theatre

Victory Over the Sun was the result of an unusual conjuncture between popular theatrical traditions and that of avant-garde theatre, the latter being well-developed in both Russia and Western Europe by the early 20th century. Various practices and conventions employed by both these traditions inspired, found expression in and were brought to fulfilment in *Victory Over the Sun*.

The libretto of the opera sets in train a series of events which are as incredulous and funny as the epic narratives (*byliny*) and fantastical folk stories (*skazki*) that have come down to us from Russian folk culture and they are acted out on stage with a vivacious sense of clowning and buffoonery. This aspect of the opera reaches back into Russian culture to the ancient tradition of the *skomorokhi*, the itinerant minstrels, clowns, actors and dancers, who passed from village to village with strange tales, side-splitting jokes and entertainments of all kinds. In the early 20th century the avant-garde became increasingly interested in the tradition of the *skomorokhi*. Susan Compton identifies references to it in the cover design of Nikolai Kulbin's book *Studia impressionistov* and we can also trace its influence in the public buffoonery of the Russian Futurists. [5]

In addition, *Victory Over the Sun* was rooted in the popular entertainments of the village fairs and the Shrovetide festivities in which mummers entertained the people by dressing as well known characters who could be cheered or jeered accordingly. Characters included musicians and actors dressed as a she-goat and a bear, Farnos the Clown, who possessed an enormous red nose and rode a pig, and Erioma, who spoke nonsense and performed feats of daring and magic. Audience participation was essential to popular Russian theatre. It was a theatre of rank enjoyment, a theatre of laughter and a theatre of the people. In early 20th century Russia, theatre directors and theorists such as Nikolai Evreinov (1879 – 1953) turned attention to these ancient forms of theatre and explored their conventions and theatrical possibilities by restaging dramatic *genres* such as mystery plays.[6]

When the rural population of Russian began to migrate to urban centres in the 19th century they took their folk theatre with them. In this new context the ancient traditions were transformed into street entertainment and circus and it was these that chiefly interested young directors such as Vsevolod Meyerkhold, who attempted to introduce their characteristics into conventional theatre. It was not only stage professionals who began to appreciate these sources but also the avant-garde. The Italian Futurists were inspired by music hall, hence Marinetti's famous 'Variety Theatre Manifesto' of 1913, which celebrated the versatility and novelty of the music hall in the face of the hidebound realism and historicism of regular theatre.[7] In addition, John Bowlt has demonstrated the importance of circus clowns and jesters for Russian artists such as Larionov and Goncharova, particularly in 1913 when they appeared in public with painted faces and bizarre hairstyles.[8]

Victory Over the Sun followed in this tradition. The apparent nonsense of the libretto, the daring events of the plot, the surprising costumes and *coups de théâtre* such as that of the first scene, in which 'two men in three-cornered hats tore the white calico drop-curtain in half', possessed all the showmanship and public appeal of the popular theatre that had preceded it.[9] No wonder that, as Benedikt Livshits says, 'the audience's attention was absorbed immediately by the spectacle before them'.[10]

The Wagnerian Revolution

In exploiting the connotations of popular theatre, *Victory Over the Sun* aligned itself with the culture of the people rather than with that of the bourgeoisie. Indeed it deliberately parodied middle-class cultural forms. This much is explicit in the fact that *Victory Over the Sun* was called an 'opera' yet point for point opposed the refined conventions of that medium. In this respect *Victory Over the Sun* was subversive and its appeal to folk traditions represented an important aspect of its oppositional agenda. Yet the aim of the opera was not simply to parody the culture and status of the bourgeoisie. In telling the tale of revolution in allegorical form the opera also questioned the traditional dominance of institutions such as the church and the monarchy. Through an appeal to popular traditions, through the use of allegory on stage and through parody of conventional theatrical forms, the opera attempted to transform the consciousness of its audience, to awaken them to the possibility of change and, if necessary, by violent means.

In this sense *Victory Over the Sun* was also grounded in Richard Wagner's revolutionary concept of theatre, and particularly music-drama, as a medium of personal, social and political transformation. In the early 20th century many avant-garde artists considered Wagner as part of the cultural status quo that they sought to oppose because he had been the darling of the Symbolist generation who were now regarded as old-fashioned and decidedly anti-modernist. However, Wagner's impact upon the arts was so great that the avant-garde could not entirely escape it. Young composers were still coming to terms with the implications of his music and despite the fashionable 'anti-Wagner' cult, many key figures in the development of early 20th century Modernism, such as Sergei Diaghilev and Vasily Kandinsky, were fired by his ideas. Indeed, the influence of Wagner was felt across the arts at this time and it was enormously significant in the Russian context as demonstrated by Rosamund Bartlett in her book, *Wagner and Russia*.[11]

It was not Wagner's long and psychologically complex plots that attracted the younger generation (though Kandinsky was inspired by his myth-making), but his concept of the revolutionary potential of the art work and his view that the transformative power of art relied upon its ability to unite music, poetry, performance and visual art to one common end. Wagner believed that by harnessing the various modes of artistic creation in one 'total art work', a *Gesamtkunstwerk*, he could operate across the senses and transform the human organism.[12] This was an attractive idea for many young people engaged in the arts at this time such as the Symbolists, Diaghilev, Meyerkhold, Kandinsky and Scriabin to name but a few who feature in Bartlett's study on the subject.[13]

Russian stage directors and theorists explored the transformative power of theatre in a variety of ways. Fedor Komissarzhevsky, on the one hand, insisted on a Wagnerian view by insisting on the unification of the arts to reveal the inner essence of a play or opera to elicit the common emotional and spiritual experience of his audience. Nikolai Evreinov, on the other, argued that all art directly influenced life but that theatre was best placed to undertake this task. In his book, *Monodrama,* of 1909 he wrote that in theatre every spectator identifies himself or herself with the protagonist on the stage, with the result that we become those characters. Compton has already demonstrated the importance of Evreinov's theories for Mayakovsky in the production of *Vladimir Mayakovsky: A Tragedy* which ran alongside *Victory Over the Sun* during its short run in December 1913.[14] It was this revolutionary understanding of the art work as a medium capable of change and transformation, grounded in Wagner and developed by subsequent theorists, that underpinned the working conception of *Victory Over the Sun.*

The Russian *Gesamtkunstwerk*

The equal participation of Malevich, Matiushin and Kruchenykh upon the project and the careful balance achieved between sound, text and image clearly locates one of the sources of the opera in the Wagnerian concept of the *Gesamtkunstwerk*. There was nothing unusual in this, however, since many avant-garde productions of the day rooted themselves in this concept. Following Wagner's death it became increasingly popular to explore the expressive possibilities afforded by the integration of the arts. The painter was seen as an indispensable participant in the theatrical projects and stage and costume design played an ever more important role in the production.

Symbolist painters such as the Nabis, and Edouard Vuillard in particular, were amongst the first to explore such interdisciplinary activity and they did so in the small avant-garde theatres of Paris such as Paul Fort's *Théâtre d'art* and Lugné-Poe's *Théâtre de l'oeuvre*. This generation of artists legitimated the practice of stage and costume design as a valid activity for the modernist painter, seeing in it not only a means of common exploration with composers and poets, but also a means of exploring aesthetic ideas in three dimensions and attracting a wider audience than could be addressed via the gallery or dealership.

It was possible, of course, to proceed independently and various composers and artists did this. Kandinsky explored the relationship between painting and music in his play *The Yellow Sound* and the composer Aleksandr Scriabin had made a significant attempt to integrate colour and sound by composing and performing on a colour organ which projected a coloured beam of light across the auditorium when a particular key was played. Attempts such as these to fuse the arts in a more cohesive manner than Wagner were widely discussed in avant-garde circles, but although inspirational and artistically significant in their own way, they were economically unsuccessful. It was, in fact, the established theatres that most consistently developed Wagner's ideas. Meyerkhold's work for Komissarzhevskaya's theatre in St. Petersburg were chiefly notable in this respect. His 1906 production of *Hedda Gabler*, for example, synchronised colours and gestures in order to evoke specific moods.

Above all it was Serge Diaghilev, impresario of The Ballets Russes, who finally brought Wagner's concept to fruition through the medium of ballet and made an economic and creative success of it. Diaghilev founded The Ballet Russes in 1909 with the intention of renovating ballet by making it a vehicle for interdisciplinary creation. Over a period of twenty years Diaghilev insisted on an intimate collaboration between the composer, artist and choreographer. [15] The remarkable integration of the arts in ballets such as the orientalist *Schéhérezade* of 1910, which matched Lev Bakst, Mikhail Fokine and Nikolai Rimsky-Korsakov; in the Primitivist *Rite of Spring* of 1912, which placed Nikolai Roerikh with Vaslav Nijinsky and Igor Stravinsky; and the Russian folk extravaganza *Le Coq d'Or* of 1914, which combined Goncharova, Fokine and Rimsky-Korsakov, had not only made his company internationally successful but had also legitimated the role of the avant-garde in theatrical innovation.

Perhaps it was the example of Vera Komissarzhevskaya and of Diaghilev that the authors of *Victory Over the Sun* had in mind when they decided to stage their opera in the Luna Park Theatre, which although recently modernised, was a relatively conventional theatrical setting. In any case, by 1913, Wagner's concept of the *Gesamtkunstwerk* represented one of the key issues that any example of Modernist theatre really had to address and *Victory Over the Sun* was no exception. The broken speech of the *zaum* libretto, the examples of quarter-tone music, the fragmented narrative, the fractured appearance of the sets and the dissolution of the theatrical space by means of coloured lights, which recall those employed by Scriabin, are evidence of the fact that the *Gesamtkunstwerk* was of crucial importance to Matiushin, Kruchenykh and Malevich. In addition, when the opening bars of the score were reproduced in the Russian Futurist book *The Three* (*Troe*), they were accompanied by the stage direction 'transition in dark-blue and black' *('perekhod v goluboe i chernoe')* which Compton sees as evidence of the synaesthetic aims of the opera.[16] Through their intimate collaboration, the authors of the opera hoped to create an integrated and expressive work through which the individual consciousness of the spectator might be radically transformed.

Towards a Modernist Theatre

It was widely believed that the expressive potential of any art work was dependent upon its degree of artistic autonomy. Kandinsky, for example, believed that colour, line and shape could only exert their full effect on the soul of the spectator when they were 'liberated' from their traditional descriptive function. Indeed, the view that art could only be truly expressive and truly itself when operating outside of mimesis became the central tenet of artistic Modernism. Mimetic approaches were considered morally disingenuous because they were geared around the concept of deceit. Indeed, many Modernist artists conflated illusionism and the means by which it masked the qualities of the medium with the flawed morality and culture of the bourgeoisie. In contrast, Modernist practices were believed to possess integrity and intellectual honesty because they rendered explicit the qualities of the medium and exposed the lie of naturalistic art. This approach inevitably possessed subversive and oppositional connotations.

In the early 20th century, European theatre was dominated by Naturalism, a theatre of illusion in which real problems and issues could be addressed through performances which mirrored reality. In Russia, Naturalism had reached its apogee in the work of Konstantin Stanislavsky, director of the Moscow Art Theatre, whose development of the 'psychological method' of acting created works of intense realism. One of the first and most potent challenges to the Naturalist tradition in Russia was undertaken by Aleksandr Blok when, in his play, *The Puppet Booth* (*Balaganchik*) of 1906, the wounded clown cries out to the audience:

'... Help!
I'm bleeding cranberry juice!
Bandaged with rags!
On my head there's a cardboard helmet!
And in my hand a wooden sword!' [17]

Here Blok questioned the illusionism upon which Naturalistic theatre was grounded. He used theatre to call attention to the very means that theatre itself employed by frankly admitting that it is, in essence, an artifice of cranberry juice and cardboard props. When Meyerkhold staged the play for Komissarzhevskaya in St. Petersburg he drew out and emphasised these very features since, like Blok, he believed that theatre was at its best when the audience remained constantly aware that they were in a theatre. To achieve this aim it was necessary to emphasise the formal characteristics of theatre. Across Europe the Symbolist generation was undertaking a similar critique of Naturalism and in the early 20th century a number of directors and impresarios took up the call to develop a Modernist theatre that would acknowledge, in the production itself, the means at its disposal and upon which the production depended. The result was to dissemble the medium and to create a conceptual form of performance that was believed to be more expressive than mimetic forms of Naturalism. *Victory Over the Sun* operates in this very vein, for when the two actors break through the calico backdrop at the start of the opera, attention is drawn to theatre itself and to the means that it adopts. This single action serves the same effect as Blok's puppet that bleeds cranberry juice and it betrays the debt to *Balaganchik*.

Evreinov was also an advocate of the Modernist stage though his views were grounded on a different premise to that of Meyerkhold. Evreinov believed that theatre is an instinctual urge and that it manifests itself in daily life. In Evreinov's system life *is* theatre and, therefore, the concept of the Naturalistic stage was illogical. In his own theatre, known as The Crooked Mirror, Evreinov staged a variety of productions that parodied, and hence deconstructed, the techniques of conventional and highly popular theatrical pieces. His production of *Vampuka*, for example, used parody to explore and render explicit the conventions of opera as reflected in Verdi's *Aida*.

By 1911 even Stanislavsky veered away from Naturalism for he invited Edward Gordon Craig to Moscow to stage a production of *Hamlet* in which Craig 'showed how music, architecture and painting could be fused into a symphonic unity'.[18] Moreover, Craig rejected the scenic Realism of conventional stage décor and used in its place a composition of screens. An expressive use of light and colour worked hand in hand with these settings and in this way Craig realised the full psychological drama of the play. Craig's arrival at the Moscow Arts Theatre demonstrates the revolutionary success of Modernist stage-craft. Even the Imperial Theatres took a bow to Modernist practices by appointing Meyerkhold as a director and, even if he was restricted in this new appointment, Meyerkhold still found opportunities to exploit his modernist views. In October 1910 Meyerkhold became the director of The House of Interludes in St. Petersburg and here the preliminaries to the theatrical performance became part of the performance itself. On occasion, the audience were used for casting, and make-up was applied in the auditorium in full view of the public.[19] All of these devices drew attention to and rendered explicit the means of theatre and it was on examples such as these that *Victory Over the Sun* was grounded.

Radical Modernism and Avant-Garde Experimentation

Nonetheless, the Modernism of the conventional theatres looked old-fashioned when compared with the experiments being undertaken by the Russian avant-garde. As early as January 1911 the Union of Youth staged a work in St. Petersburg entitled *Mansion House Scenes* (*Khoromniya Deistva*), which drew upon and developed Modernist approaches to the stage.[20] This production featured the restaging of a traditional folk play entitled *Tsar Maksem'ian and his Disobedient Son Adolf*. This play comprised a collection of scenes with no unified narrative, since traditional folk performances of this play had themselves abandoned logic and realism and engaged in shifts of time and space. In this respect *Mansion House Scenes* was a forerunner of *Victory Over the Sun*, which likewise comprised a series of largely unrelated events featuring diverse characters in improbable meetings.

Jeremy Howard comments upon the archaic connotations of the folk costumes, of the décor, based upon *lubok* sources, and of the use of amateur actors on a *balagan* stage. In addition to the play, *Mansion House Scenes* also comprised traditional Russian folk dances, games and parodies of high culture in which the audience were encouraged to participate as actors. In short, '*Khoromniya Deistva* essentially comprised a rejection of contemporary theatre and technique. The return to traditional folk methods and acts served to highlight the desire for change and formal innovation and to act as a highly significant precedent for *Victory Over the Sun*.'[21]

Mansion House Scenes represented the first expression in avant-garde circles of all the diverse trends and concepts of theatrical modernism that were then circulating in Russia. The sources lay not only in the ancient folk traditions of popular theatre but were also derived from Meyerkhold's ideas about circus, cabaret and audience involvement as well as those of Evreinov, who promoted the idea of ancient theatrical forms in the face of theatrical realism. In adopting this novel form of theatre the Union of Youth made a telling critique of bourgeois values and culture and promoted in their place that 'other' culture, the culture of the people.

In Moscow, the most decisive headway in reforming stage practice was made by Natalia Goncharova and Mikhail Larionov. In 1913 these two artists had established contact with Evreinov and had adopted his concept of 'the theatricalisation of life' by appearing in public with painted faces.[22] In his manifesto, 'Why We Paint Ourselves', of December 1913, Larionov explained:

> We have joined art to life. After the long isolation of artists, we have loudly summoned life and life has invaded art, it is time for art to invade life. The painting of our faces is the start of the invasion.[23]

Theatre was the medium by which this invasion was to be achieved and in addition to this inventive form of street theatre the two artists also took their ideas onto the stage.

In early September Larionov and Goncharova announced their intention to open a Futurist theatre in Moscow called *Teatr Futu*, which entertained nothing less than a subversion of conventional theatre:

> What serves as the stalls in non-futurist theatres will represent the stage. The audience will be placed, depending on the action, either on a dais in the middle of the theatrical hall or over it, on a constructed wire net under the ceiling. In the latter case it will be necessary to watch the play from above, through the mesh of the rack, lying or squatting, whichever is more comfortable.[24]

In addition, Larionov proposed to remove all the props from the stage and to replace them with actors:

> The actors themselves will play the props and costumes. So there will be the actor-hat, the actor-trousers, the actor-handkerchief, the actor-boots, the actor-table, -door, -window etc. In general, Futurist theatre will not be theatre performing plays but theatre performing theatre.[25]

Hence Larionov arrived at a form of theatre which represented the logical conclusion of the Modernist agenda, and in this he was truly radical.

The Russian press published detailed plans for the staging of Goncharova's and Larionov's repertoire. Goncharova, for example, entertained a system of 'inverse perspective' for her production of Hoffmanstahl's *Les noces de Zobeide* and *Le Bedeau*.[26] Larionov considered more radical measures. In his staging of Konstantin Bolshakov's *Jig of the Streets* (*Pliaska ulits*), in which the hero was to be performed by three actors in different settings simultaneously, Larionov was reported to have designed three sets, a restaurant, an apartment and the street outside, and to have placed them one behind the other.[27] A similar approach was adopted for the play *Dust, Street Dust* (*Pyl, ulitsy pyl*) written by Anton Lotov. [28] In addition, Larionov planned to abandon the seamless mimesis of Naturalist theatre by emphasising the processes of theatre in the scene changes:

> … the sets will be brought in on one side, while the old sets are pulled off on the other. This will take place gradually, not quickly, so that at a given moment the stage will have two, three or even four sets crossing in front of each other'.[29]

Techniques such as these represented an apotheosis of Modernism since theatre was performing theatre.

In October 1913 Goncharova and Larionov finally opened their Futurist theatre and called it The Pink Lantern (Rozovy fonar). Here they would organise Futurist evenings, paint the faces of audience members and entertain and abuse the crowd. On the opening evening, however, there was a public riot and The Pink Lantern was closed by the police.[30] It appears, therefore, that none of the projected performances took place. Nonetheless, Larionov's theoretical radicalism set a precedent for Russian avant-garde theatre and it was his example that was uppermost in the minds of the *Victory Over the Sun* team as they prepared their opera. In a letter to Matiushin of 11 September 1913, Malevich urged his colleagues to complete the opera as soon as possible to forestall Larionov from anticipating their première with his 'Rayist theatre'.[31]

The fear of being literally 'upstaged' was no idle one since, according to one report, Larionov planned to open his 'Futurist Theatre' at The Pink Lantern with décor and staging that would move, with music and lighting that would conform to the dancing and that the plays would be 'beyond the limits of the language of ideas, being a free and invented onomatopoeia'.[32] To all intents and purposes, Larionov's plays, which intended to combine the various elements of theatre and which hinged around a *zaum* libretto, would have cut the ground from underneath *Victory Over the Sun*.

Larionov and Goncharova might have achieved their ends had they not secured a contract to star in a Futurist film entitled *Drama in the Futurists' Cabaret No. 13* and had Diaghilev not invited Goncharova to design the sets and costumes for his forthcoming production of *Le Coq d'Or* at the Paris Opéra. Both these commissions so completely absorbed Larionov and Goncharova that the way was clear for Malevich, Kruchenykh and Matiushin to achieve in practice that of which Larionov had only dreamed.

The Essence of *Victory*

The opera *Victory Over the Sun* made a deliberate appeal to the popular traditions of the Russian theatre, which opposed those of the bourgeoisie. It was conceived in a post-Wagnerian frame of reference, which insisted on the transformative power of theatre through the unification of the arts on the stage. It was rooted in the debates and practices of the Modernist stage in which the means of theatre were made explicit in the performance, hence opposing the beloved Naturalist theatre of the establishment. It rooted itself in and was legitimated by the innovations of Diaghilev, Komissarzhevsky, Meyerkhold and Evreinov but it was no pastiche of these for it condensed them according to the example of Goncharova and Larionov. In so doing, *Victory Over the Sun* created a revolutionary form of stage practice. Professional acting was banished from the stage, Naturalism was opposed, and the traditional principles of costume and set design, of lighting, music and libretto were inverted in the same way as the backdrops in the contemporary photographs of Malevich, Matiushin and Kruchenykh (in Volume 1).

Victory Over the Sun expressed its revolutionary message through an equally revolutionary stagecraft that opposed point for point the theatre of the bourgeoisie and by implication bourgeois culture as a whole and the establishment for which it stood. The concept of 'tearing down' the old to make way for the new is a central metaphor of the operatic narrative. It is present in the tearing of the calico curtain and in the tearing of the sun from the sky.[33] But the concept of 'tearing down' was also implicit in the revolutionary form of the opera for, at a stroke, it tore down the firmament of bourgeois culture and, to use Malevich's words, making a bag of it, stuffed in all the conventional approaches to art, music, literature and theatre itself, and tied it with a knot. All that remained to its creators was 'the white free chasm' – infinity was before them and the comrade aviators gaily sailed towards it.[34] Thirty years after Wagner's death, the 'art work of the future' had finally arrived but it was not quite as he had predicted. *Victory Over the Sun* was as wild and headstrong as a *muzhik* and just as dangerous, for it spoke of revolution and not just in the aesthetic sense.

Notes

1   *Genesis*, 1: 14-16.

2   F. T. Marinetti, *Uccidiamo il chiaro di luna* (Milan, Edizione Futuriste di Poesie 1911).

3   See *Revelation*, 6:12-13 and 10:6. At the opening of the Sixth Seal the sun turns black as sackcloth, the moon turns red as blood, the stars fall from the sky and the heavens and earth are rolled up like a scroll.

4   B. Livshits, *Polutoraglazy strelets* (1933), translated into English by John E. Bowlt, *The One and a Half-Eyed Archer* (Newtonville: Oriental Research Partners, 1977), 163-164. In Volume 1 of this collection.

5   Susan Compton, *The World Backwards: Russian Futurist Books 1912–1916* (London: British Library, 1978), 46-47.

6   Evreinov's chief publication in the years before the First World War was *Teatr kak takovoi* (St. Petersburg: Sovremennoe iskusstva, 1912).

7   F. T. Marinetti, *Il teatro di varietà* (Milan: Direzione del movimento futurista 1913).

8   See John E. Bowlt, 'Natalia Goncharova and Futurist Theatre', *Art Journal*, Vol. 49, No. 1 (Spring 1990), 44-51.

9   Livshits, [4], *The One and a Half-Eyed Archer*, 162, and in Volume 1.

10   Ibid.

11   R. Bartlett, *Wagner and Russia* (Cambridge: Cambridge University Press, 1995).

12   Richard Wagner, 'Art and Revolution' (*Die Kunst und die Revolution*), 1849, vol. III, 8-41; 'The Art Work of the Future' (*Das kunstwerk der Zukunft*), 1849, vol. I, 194-206; and 'Opera and Drama' (*Oper und Drama*), 1852, Vol. III, 222-320 & Vol. IV, 1-229, all volumes of Wagner, *Sämtliche Schriften und Dichtungen* (Leipzig: Breitkopf & Härtel, 1912–1914).

13   Bartlett, *Wagner and Russia* [11].

14   Compton, *The World Backwards* [5], 48-51.

15   K. Bazarov, 'Diaghilev and the Radical Years of Modern Art', *Art and Artists*, Vol. 10, No. 4 (July 1975), 6-15.

16   Compton, *The World Backwards* [5], 53-54.

17   *Balaganchik* was first written by Blok as a poem in July 1905 and then transposed into the form of a play.

18   M. Slonim, *Russian Theatre from the Empire to the Soviets* (London: Methuen, 1963), 158.

19   Jeremy Howard, *The Union of Youth. An Artists' Society of the Russian Avant-Garde* (Manchester: Manchester University Press, 1992), 75.

20   *Mansion House Scenes* opened on 27 January 1911. For further discussion of this event see Howard, *The Union of Youth,* Ibid.

21   Ibid., 85-86.

22   Goncharova and Larionov made their first public appearance with painted faces on Kuztnetsky Most in Moscow in September 1913. The contemporary Russian press records many such events. The first is discussed in 'Vcherashniaia progulka futuristov', *Stolichnaia molva*, 15 September 1913, No. 327, 4 and 'Raskrashennyi Larionov', *Moskovskaia gazeta*, 9 September 1913, No. 272, 3; and 'Rakrashennye moskvichi', 15 September 1913, No. 273, 5 and 16 September 1913, No. 274, 5.

23   M. Larionov and I. Zdanevich, 'Pochemu my raskrashivaemsia: Manifest futuristov', *Argus*, Christmas 1913, 115-18.

24   'Teatr Futu', *Moskovskaia gazeta*, 9 September 1913, No. 272, 5.

25   Ibid.

26   V. Parnack, *Gontcharowa. Larionow: L'art Décoratif Théâtral Moderne* (Paris: Edition 'La Cible', 1919), 10 and 16.

27   'Futuristicheskaia drama', *Stolichnaia molva*, 7 October 1913, No. 331, 4.

28   'Proekt M. F. Larionova dlia stseny v futuristicheskom teatre k piese Lotova *Pyl'ulitsy pyl'*, *Teatr v karrikaturakh*, 29 September 1913, No. 4, 8. It is likely that this play was one and the same as *Pliaska ulits* since the descriptions of the three stages are very similar.

29   Ibid.

30   For a full discussion of Larionov's and Goncharova's theatre and cinematographic work see A. Parton, *Mikhail Larionov and the Russian Avant-Garde* (Princeton: Princeton University Press, 1993).

31   N. Khardzhiev, 'Is materialov o Maiakovskom', *30 dnei*, No. 7 (1939), 82-85.

32   'K proektu futuristicheskogo teatra v Moskve', *Teatr v karrikaturkakh*, 8 September 1913, No. 1, 14.

33   The tearing of the calico curtain parodies the tearing of the curtain in the temple following the crucifixion of Christ and suggests the coming of the new order. See Matthew, 27:51; Mark, 15:38 and Luke, 23:45.

34   K. S. Malevich, *Essays on Art – Vol. 1 1915–1933* (London: Rapp & Whiting, 1969), 122.

Nina Gourianova

ALEKSEI KRUCHENYKH'S THEATRE OF ALOGISM

Between 1913 and 1916 Aleksei Kruchenykh wrote several plays and short dramatic pieces, including *Victory Over the Sun* in 1913 (*Pobeda nad solntsem*). It was directed by the author and staged by the First Futurist Theatre in December of the same year.

Another opera, *The Military Opera* (*Voennaia opera*), which he started together with Khlebnikov in 1914, remained unfinished and exists only in draft form, but it is no less important for the history of Russian Futurism. Kruchenykh's '*deiuga*', or drama, *The Bridge* (*Most*), was written around the turn of 1913 – 1914, 'after *Victory*' and before '*The Military Opera*', according to the author himself.[1] Even this brief remark seems to indicate that Kruchenykh may have regarded this short play not as an independent work but as something intermediate and 'relative to' his two 'major' plays that were written with a certain amount of involvement from Khlebnikov. In addition, there is a brief drama scene in one act (*Deimo*) from his book, *Let's Grumble* (*Vozropshchem*, 1913), and *Gly-Gly*, an unfinished play about Futurism and Futurists (1915 – 1916).[2] Because all of them are linked chronologically and stylistically and were written in the key of early Futurist poetics and *alogism*, I think it is possible to speak of *Kruchenykh's theatre*.

Unfortunately, this theme has hardly been addressed in the literature on Futurism. To the extent that Kruchenykh is mentioned at all in the context of early Futurist theatre, it is only in connection with *Victory Over the Sun*, which is sometimes incorrectly regarded as his only and more or less incidental experiment in the dramatic genre.

Nonetheless, judging by Kruchenykh's memoirs and the reminiscences of his contemporaries, he showed a consistent and professional interest in the theatre – in particular Vsevolod Meyerkhold's experiments – since being a student in 1905 – 1906. While he was in Kherson, he regularly published theatre reviews in a local newspaper. Later, Kruchenykh became known for his outstanding histrionic talent and he had the voice of a professional actor; his masterful performance of poetry reading was often remarked upon. And he didn't just write *Victory Over the Sun* – he directed it, and played two roles in it – A Certain Person with Bad Intentions and A Reader.

Language and Alogism

What distinguished Kruchenykh's vision of theatre as an individual, independent phenomenon from other contemporary or earlier tendencies stylistically related to it (for example, that of Alfred Jarry or Nikolai Evreinov), was above all its novel approach to language and the sound texture of the text. Sometimes the characters in his play resort to pure sound poetry (e.g. the 'petty bourgeois song' of A Young Man in *Victory Over the Sun*), while in other cases we find morphological license or semantic shifts.

In Kruchenykh's plays language is intentionally transformed into the principal 'artistic event', serving as the *subject* of art more than a *means* of communication or instrument for characterization; sometimes it turns into phonic noise background for the pantomime going on on-stage. As he created his theory of *zaum* (or *transrational* language, better translated as "beyonsense" by American poet and Khlebnikov's translator, Paul Schmidt) between 1912 and 1915, Kruchenykh took a deep interest in scientific studies of the unconscious and of intuition – particularly Sigmund Freud's theory of language and the unconscious. He also studied the latest research on the «speaking in tongues» of sectarians and the transrational revelations during religious services of the Khlysty and Old Believers. He gradually came to produce his own version of the anti-literary canon (or rejection of the closed grammatical structure of the written language) and turned to the nature of speech, its objective properties and physical phonic aspects. It is the phonic texture of the language that comes to the fore in his plays in the incorporation of a chorus and glossolalia, devices that subsequently became distinguishing features of 20th century experimental theatre.

Thus, Ilya Zdanevich was developing his 'polyphonic creation' of 'multi-poetry' to convey 'our many faced and split existence' in his plays of the 1920s. In his search, Zdanevich concentrated on the category of sound, but found a unique visual form for his text, structured almost like a musical score, to reflect the polysemous chords of the truly 'symphonic' sound of his dramas: 'Correcting our defective mouths, we have come to orchestral poetry, speaking in crowds and everything different.... And multi-poetry, which you cannot read silently,... runs flushed onto the stage to take the trenches by storm....'[3] The same principles dominate the theatre of Antonin Artaud, which undermines the utilitarianism of language and attempts to use speech like a magic spell to restore its ability to shock physically.[4] Not coincidentally, this aspect of Kruchenykh's theatre antecedes the later tendencies in surrealist theatre and the postwar theatre of the absurd. This comparison, maybe unexpected for some, of the 'theatre of alogism' with the theatre of the absurd can be easily justified by Eugene Ionesco's notion that the themes of the absurd '... can be found throughout the history of the theatre'.[5] Much as Malevich's Suprematism is connected in retrospect with the history of the staging of *Victory Over the Sun*, Kruchenykh's theatre of alogism lives on in the later stages of the avant-garde, above all, of course, in Ilya Zdanevich's notion of '*transrational* theatre', and in Daniil Kharms' surrealistic phantasmagories, particularly his early plays, *The Comedy of the City of Petersburg* and *The Paw (Lapa)*.[6]

The conception of the play is especially reminiscent of the stylistics of performance as found in Italian Futurism and Zurich Dada. The lines of the characters are written as a 'score', and the sound, rhythm, and tempo of the text are extremely important (cf. Kruchenykh's stage directions: 'sings', 'shouts', 'squeaks', 'crash', etc.).

It is quite remarkable that Kruchenykh divided his plays, as he did his transrational poetry, into 'mute' works (for publication), and those intended to be performed – 'for sound'. In a letter from Tiflis to the poet Sergei Gorodetsky in which he may be referring both to *Gly-Gly* (which Kruchenykh tentatively intended to publish in the never-realised journal *Supremus*), and *The Bridge*, he noted: 'I have some plays here – one for publication, and another for performance'.[7]

Kruchenykh's theory of transrational language coincided in time with the emergence of *Alogism* in the visual arts, which was introduced by Malevich and quickly adopted by his Futurist brothers-in-arms. The style of Kruchenykh's early plays of 1913 and 1914, it seems to me, are no exception and are more than anything consistent with this *principle of alogism*, structured on dissonance, as enunciated by Malevich on the back of his painting *Cow and Violin* (now in the State Russian Museum in St. Petersburg) in 1913: 'The alogical juxtaposition ... of forms ... as an element of the struggle against logic, naturalism, philistine meaning, and prejudice'.

Indeed, the semantic connections between Kruchenykh's dramatic characters, in essence, are the same as those between objects in Malevich's *alogical* paintings of 1913 and 1914. (It is the ironic and theatricalized, or 'playful' character of these compositions that became one of the pivotal elements in *alogism*.) In *Cow and Violin* (1913), *Englishman in Moscow* (1914, reproduced on page 96 herein), or *Aviator* (1914, State Russian

Museum), for example, within the painterly composition there is a *transrational* 'riddle' made up of what at first seem to be random objects and fragments offered to the viewer as a kind of game.[8] In this game, however, there is no 'prize', no absolute solution, or single correct answer, since the riddle does not lend itself to rational logic.

The connection between these details – objects and persons – taken out of their usual context and therefore deprived of any real content and open to any interpretation, is irrational, free, and associative. The meaning and sense of each of them is mobile and ambivalent, slipping away and changing, depending on the context. Objects in these constructions are like words in *transrational* poetry – they can accumulate a whole gamut of meanings, from everyday details to metaphysical symbols. And the author – poet or painter – may be prompting several levels of interpretation, grounded in a play on words and free associations.

Metaphor of War

Kruchenykh named his play *Victory Over Sun* and, from the very beginning, presented his reader and spectator with a 'riddle' or 'Futurist trick', of which Kruchenykh was a Grand Master. Victory presupposes a war, and 'war' in the early Russian avant-garde was semantically complex and more of a metaphor than a subject. One can say that Kruchenykh wrote his drama 'by means of war' (by analogy with ink), using war not as a subject but as a medium and metaphor for Futurist creativity: if Marinetti strived to 'kill the moonlight', Kruchenykh and Malevich forged the attack on the *'sun of the iron age'*. In an interview with the newspaper *Day (Den)*, Matiushin and Malevich explained what *Victory Over the Sun* was about, saying:

> The meaning of the opera has to do with the overthrow of one of the great artistic values – in this particular case, the sun.... In the consciousness of man human thought has established certain connections between them.
> The Futurists want to free themselves from this ordered quality of the world, from the connections thought to exist in it. They want to transform the world into chaos, to smash the established values to pieces and from these pieces create new values by making new generalizations and discovering new, unexpected and invisible connections. Take the sun – this is a former value – it therefore constrains them, and they want to overthrow it.[9]

The metaphor of *war* was connected to the idea of innovation, the idea of destroying old forms and the old aesthetics for the sake of creating anew. In his discussion of contemporary art, Kandinsky once called it 'truly anarchistic' in the sense that it 'embodies the spirit as a materializing force, ripe for revelation'.[10] This theme of aesthetic anarchy and unbound, creative freedom, understood as the freedom from metaphysical rationality, goes together with the idea of the intensity, and symbolic 'violence', of creation. Ever since creating *Victory Over Sun,* the anarchic features of Kruchenykh's poetics – the intensity of the nihilist artistic gesture, the poetics of absurdism, and resistance to all the common values – move him towards foreshadowing the problematics of Dadaism and Surrealism. In a sense, *Victory* is dedicated to the death of God, or rather, to the 'death of the myth of modernity', which inspired shock in some minds and liberated others:

> I want to say everything – recollect the past full of the sorrows of mistakes... the breaking and bending of knees... let us remember it and compare it with the present... so joyous: liberated from the heaviness of universal gravity we can imaginatively arrange our belongings as if a rich kingdom were being moved. (Scene 5)

This drama is a contemporary anti-utopia, one that closes in proclaiming that *'the world will perish but to us there is no end!'.* The very title of Kruchenykh's play reveals something that is beyond the human world, turning the notion of progress and of human history into a small, insignificant detail. In the works of Dadaists we find the same point of view regarding the world – an anti-teleological perspective that demonstrates the absurdity of human existence, when the only truth and the only reality that remains is the reality of art, of the word.

In *Victory* this reality is in discord with the persistent routine of aesthetic, social and ideological dogmas and clichés; it resists any hierarchical structure and utopian way of thinking by means of parody, of dissonance, of the philosophical 'openness' of nihilism, and of the displacement of aesthetic and social ideologies.

The same anarchic inspiration that drives Kruchenykh to the language of 'beyonsense' was at the roots of the nihilism of Suprematism, Malevich's aesthetic theory of the 'void', of nothingness. Malevich once said that the black square symbolised the beginning of *victory* in Kruchenykh's play. And in this context, Maurice Blanchot's reading of nihilism as the 'permission to know all'[11] seems to correspond most closely to Kruchenykh's and Malevich's idea of nothingness and infinity.

Parody and Provocation

Kruchenykh's work is not a drama or libretto in the usual sense of the word. Yet in contrast to the other Futurist play performed along with *Victory*, Mayakovsky's tragedy, *Vladimir Mayakovsky*, none of Kruchenykh's plays can by any means be regarded as a lyrical poem in drama form. On the contrary, it is from the outset intended to be acted, and deliberate scenic effects are specifically indicated in the text. It transcends genre definitions. The principle of *alogism,* or dissonance, suggests a complete disintegration of idea, text, and traditional staging.

In his memoirs Kruchenykh mentioned that he was trying to create 'public theatre', to directly address, provoke and involve the audience; the theatre that would go beyond the usual entertainment, education, or moralistic lesson.

In the deliberate transcendence of genre and eclectic theatricality of *Victory* there is a touch of the variety theatre, of the circus-like, buffoonish grotesque and, to take a concrete example, the 'theatre of parody' of Koz'ma Prutkov, whom Kruchenykh much admired. The aspiration to exist outside genre boundaries and the attraction to the 'minor format' is evident in those years in the enormous popularity of cabarets, including The Bat (Letuchiaia Mysh', 1908 – 1922) and The Stray Dog (Brodiachaia Sobaka, 1911 – 1915) which caught the attention of the Futurists. And in this connection we should not forget The Crooked Mirror, Nikolai Evreinov's theatre of literary and artistic parody, which in 1913 successfully staged short plays (usually three or four in an evening). For the sake of our discussion, noteworthy among them were, *A Solemn Public Meeting in Memory of Koz'ma Prutkov* (*Torzhestvennoe publichnoe zasedanie pamiati Koz'ma Prutkova*) and the famous opera spoof *Vampuka* – 'a real fillip on the nose of theatrical humdrum', as Evreinov called it.[12] On 29 January 1914, less than two months after the Futurist performances in the Luna Park theatre, The Crooked Mirror included in one of its programs *A Butterfly Sausage* (*Kolbasa iz babochek*), a parody of Futurist theatre by N. G. Smirnov and S. S. Shcherbakov, well known parodists who collaborated with Evreinov.

The genre of parody, however, was regarded in avant-garde circles as above all an artistic form that facilitated unmasking, singling out, and simplifying 'to the point of absurdity' – in brief, the distillation of new stylistic elements and devices. In the early 1910s the crisis in the conventional theatre was painfully obvious to all, a situation that was reflected in various theoretical and practical attempts to create a new conception of the theatre and theatrical performance. These included Meyerkhold and his 'stylized theatre', Viacheslav Ivanov's mystical theatre, and Evreinov's 'theatre as such' or 'total theatre', and finally the 'fourth wall' of Stanislavsky's Moscow Art Theatre.

Incidentally, the Futurists' attitude towards the latter was unambiguously expressed by Kruchenykh in *Let's Grumble* in a laconic foreword to his short drama fragment published there: '... I haven't been to the theatre for quite some while; the last time I was there I sprained my arm fleeing from a venerable haven of vulgarity – the tinseled Art Theatre (Moscow). The new theatre gets on the nerves of habit and offers our new revelations in all the arts!'[13]

Evreinov's proclaimed thesis on 'the impotence of language in the matter of final definitions' in order to justify the pre-aesthetic essence of theatre free from literature and aesthetics, is *contra* beauty for beauty's sake and *pro* acting for acting's sake.[14] His ideas could not but appeal to the Futurists, with whose circle Evreinov was close at one time. The early Futurist literary manifestos in some respects echo Evreinov's ideas. For example, his notion that in art, form becomes content, not *vice versa*, is similar to Kruchenykh's thesis in 'New Ways of the Word' (in this Volume) that 'new form creates new content', and Evreinov's 'theatre as such' recalls the Futurists' 'word as such'. The contemporaries of The Crooked Mirror, which started its existence as a cabaret, perceived the main current in theatre to be a synthetic scenic miniature combining text, music, and dance 'without any official classification into genres'.[15]

Kruchenykh's play 'balances' on the border between theatrical and poetic manifesto on the one hand, and a parody of this manifesto on the other. It undoubtedly follows the poetics of the meta-parody regenerated in *The Puppet Booth* (*Balaganchik*), where Aleksandr Blok contextualized the ideas of the 'Argonauts' and Symbolist clichés. Of course, it is just one of the many levels of interpretation of these works, but in this particular context, *Victory* may be read as a metaphorical and self-ironic parody of Futurism. Specifically, it recalls a few theses of Kruchenykh's Futurist manifestos, which leads to the suspicion that there are a couple of images in the play – A Reader, An Aviator, A Traveller Through All Centuries – with a strong self-referential aspect.

This manner of ironic provocation in the mini-drama, *The Bridge,* for example, is even stronger than in *Victory Over the Sun*. The name of the main character – *Krivliaka* (which could be translated as *Twister*) – hints at Kruchenykh's own name (related to the verbs *twist, twirl, roll, whirl*), and he was known for playing on the semantics and etymology of his surname, creating endless 'variations on a theme': Kruch, Kruchina, Kruchenyi, and so on. The genealogy of this persona – or the easily recognizable 'playing' Nietzschean poet – is complex. Its roots go back to Blok's Pierrot played by Meyerkhold, or even more to the mask of Evreinov's Harlequin, with his love of theatrical props and twisting affectation, and the sense of total 'theatricality'.

The story line of Krivliaka-Twister, who accidentally destroys the bridge in the short play of the same title, can also be discerned in the Futurist aesthetics of *Victory Over the Sun*, and, in this respect, the heroes of the new – the Traveller and the Aviator – may be considered his prototypes.[16] The metaphor of the airplane attracted many 20th century artists and poets, especially the Futurists. David Burliuk once mentioned that Khlebnikov became interested in aviation from the point of view of 'verbal creativity'. Vasily Kamensky was a pilot. Malevich created several drawings of airplanes, including his famous painting, *Aviator* (1914). Perhaps the symbolism of the airplane in part represented the freedom 'to know it all', the blatant attempt to overcome gravity and transgress the traditional limits of space and time.

In *Victory*, the bridge is destroyed by the Aviator falling from the airplane; he himself is not hurt, but, significantly, it kills a woman: '*z... z... it's knocking it's knocking a woman has been crushed a bridge has been knocked over'.* (Scene 6) This motif[17] brings us back to one of the basic ideas of Italian Futurism, namely the Futurist heroics of the 'manly' golden age that, on a metaphorical level, conquers the passive 'effeminacy' and 'lunar beauty' of the Silver Age of Symbolism, which by 1914 had become as hackneyed as 'the silver and other azure vistas'.

However, the raw aggression of Italian Futurism turns into 'power without abuse' in the Russian context of the opera (Scene 1), and the attack is directed against the cultural banalities and social stereotypes, applied to gender, rather than gender itself. Matiushin defined the basic Futurist theme of *Victory Over the Sun* as the mockery 'of the old Romanticism and verbose windiness' and a 'victory' over the usual old notions of 'beauty' and 'art for art's sake', beneath which there isn't a living thing'.[18] Many theatrical innovators were hostile to the preponderance of melodramas and plays about 'the power of sex', 'the secrets of love' and adultery, during the years 1907 – 1917, yet the uncompromising poetry and dramaturgy of early Futurism truly did introduce 'new content' by categorically rejecting the emotional element, psychologism, and the notion of 'character development' – in Artaud's phrase, the entire 'psychological and human stagnation' of the early 20th century theatre.[19]

Perhaps that is why as soon as the Aviator appears on stage he happens to destroy the 'bridge', together with the laws of gravity and linear time, the connecting link between past and future. Without even realising it, he breaks established connections and in the purity of his behavior literally 'burns his bridges' behind him. The nihilistic pose of denial-destruction-dissonance in Kruchenykh's plays barely conceals the major theme of the emergence or birth of the new reality. For example, the appearance of the 'newborn' world as the direct result of the destruction of the bridge in *Victory* creates the overturned world, world without end, 'worldbackwards'.[20]

> all is well that
> begins well
> > and has no end
> the world will perish but to us there is no
> > > end!

These final lines of the opera almost literally repeat the first lines of the play, coming together in a perfect – *endless* – circular structure:

> > First [Strongman]
> All is well that begins well!
> > Second [Strongman]
> And ends?
> > 1st
> There will be no end!

Alogism and the Absurd

In the syncretic performance of Kruchenykh's alogical play – which includes elements of drama, lyrical poetry, melodeclamation, singing, pantomime, and abstract scenic effects – theatrical reality, like the reality of transrational words, is devoid of any communicative, utilitarian function; it not only prevails but becomes self-sufficient.

The unexpectedness of the *zaum* and phonic noises interspersed in 'correct' language shock the spectators (or readers) into a desired state of anxious indefiniteness or '*weightlessness'*, evoking uncertainty as to their notions about reality. Kruchenykh's idea, I think, was to 'infuse' or blend the fantastic element into reality, and in so doing 'get on the nerves of habit' and generate a new, alogical 'context'. Two decades later a similar principle for creating a 'new spiritual order', that would give new meaning to everyday objects, would find full expression in Antonin Artaud's theory of theatre.[21]

Discernible in Kruchenykh's play are several levels of text corresponding to various levels of reality. Its linguistic structure and phonic texture are eclectic and extremely complex consisting of recitative, melodeclamation, singing, and noises. The semantic level includes hidden quotations (including some from Kruchenykh's works and the Futurist manifestos), pseudo-proverbs, contemporary slang, Futurist neologisms juxtaposed with anachronisms, and so on. An element of the incomprehensible that is therefore alarming and, to one degree or another, shocks the spectator, is present not only in the absence of a plot, psychology, motives for the characters' behavior and character development in the traditional sense, but also in the glossolalia and linguistic dissonance that Kruchenykh is deliberately counting upon for this effect.

This theme – dissonance and destruction or the *absurd* (it is interesting that the theatre scholar, Martin Esslin, who first proposed this term for the new current in postwar theatre, underscores the original meaning of the word, that is, the absence of harmony, or *dis-harmony* in music)[22] – is at the core of Kruchenykh's early poetics. It transcends not only the boundaries of modern aesthetic doctrines but also the entire structure of the binary oppositions 'thesis – antithesis', 'plus – minus', 'black – white', 'ugly – beautiful', etc., that have traditionally been considered the basis for all balance or harmony. In Kruchenykh's works it is a question of a mixture rather than a 'synthesis', of chaos rather than balanced harmony. The shock produced by the destruction of the usual 'order of things' puts the spectator, according to one of the characters, A Fat Man, into a state of logical 'weightlessness'. (Scene 6)

In this poetics of dissonance and the dehumanization of art,[23] Kruchenykh's theatre of alogism approaches very close indeed to the surrealistic magic of Artaud's 'theatre of cruelty',[24] and certain tenets of the postwar theatre of the absurd: 'To find a form that accommodates the mess, that is the task of the artist now'.[25]

The Poetics of Play

As in the theatre of the absurd, the absence of identification of the spectator with the characters in Kruchenykh's alogical theatre brings to the fore not emotional empathy with the heroes but experience of the process of the action, sharpening the effect of its all-subsuming reality, its *super-* (or *sur-*) reality,[26] the effect of *presence* that exists outside of any linearly ordered physical time.

This reality of presence unfolding in the space of the performance or play is connected with yet another aspect that is common to both the theatre of the absurd and alogism. A 'play principle', based on a blending of the imagined and the real and the incorporation of fantastic details into an everyday context, includes an active element of irony. As for Kruchenykh's theatre – unlike, for instance, that of his contemporary Evreinov – it is not so much the embodiment of a total theatricality of life or 'theatre as such', as it is a model of free and spontaneous 'play as such' – in this case, 'playing theatre'.

This *play principle* suffuses the stylistics of early Russian Futurism and becomes an instrument of self-awareness and self-identification for the author as a 'player'.

The poetics of alogism is governed by the chaos of the intuitive and the rational, the accidental and spontaneous as play. For Kruchenykh, Khlebnikov, Malevich, and the early Mayakovsky, the process of play – whether in theatre, poetry, or in their everyday routine – can be compared to meditation as a means of achieving union with the rationally unknowable. Speaking of the role of play in society, Hans-Georg Gadamer noted that the attraction of play or a game is that it masters the players, subjugating them to itself and dictating their actions, not the other way round. According to him, play and art are similar, since both the game and the work of art possess their own essence that is independent of the consciousness of 'the players': '… in as much as nature is without purpose or intention, just as it is without exertion, it is a constantly self-renewing play, and can therefore appear as a model for art'.[27]

What directs the action of the artist-player is the process of play (and, by analogy, the creative process) – its rhythm, which exists apart from any goal or purpose, 'without why', according to its own laws, unpredictable, unrepeatable and momentary. On a certain level, play grows into a dynamic and unforeseeable model of esoteric being, or mode of life. 'Despite all of its "senselessness", the world of the artist is more *rational and real* than the world of the philistine, even in the philistine sense',[28] Kruchenykh wrote in *Let's Grumble*. In the space of alogism it is impossible and unnecessary to explain the inexplicable or transfer the unconscious into the sphere of consciousness and rational logic, since the *process* of play will always be inexplicable and unjustified from the point of view of everyday pragmatic logic and common sense. The point is that the very 'logic' (or rather the 'alogism') of play, like that of any creative process, is the logic of the absurd, of dreams and the unconscious.

If the desire to incarnate or materialise the unconscious and break free of the burden of the deeply concealed 'shadows' of the self by exorcising and driving them out of one's being is the basis of any creative process, then that process can be regarded as a ritual.[29]

In early Russian Futurism, this aspect of creativity – whether action or meditation, event or experience – is essentially far more important than the work or final product of experience in its fixed and immutable 'thingness'. The opera, directed by Kruchenykh, began with a gesture that is aggressive and purely anarchist in its intensity: a white curtain adorned with the Futurist 'hieroglyph' portraits of its creators, Malevich, Matiushin, and Kruchenykh, is ripped from bottom to top by two characters. In this symbolic beginning, which defies any closure, Kruchenykh's Theatre of Alogism reflects the same aspiration to convey through action and acting the experience of chance, the moment, and infinity.

Notes

1   For more on Kruchenykh's plays *The Military Opera* and *The Bridge* see Nina Gourianova, 'Nevdannyi Most ili Teatr Alogizma Alekseia Kruchenykh' in *Terentevskii Sbornik, 2 (*Moscow: Gileia, 1997), 324-345.

2   After a hiatus, Kruchenykh once again turned to dramaturgy in the late 1920s, writing and publishing several plays and a few sketches for drama and screenplays. These late works lie outside the thematic and chronological framework of the present study.

3   Ilya Zdanevich, *Mnogovaia poeziia.* Manuscript (1914). Archive of the State Russian Museum, St. Petersburg, f.177, doc. 22.

4   Kharms' theatre is another example: 'Kruchenykh mentions recitation ('the texture of recitation'), meaning declamation, singing, the chorus, orchestra, and so on. This is also very important for Kharms.' See Zh.-F. Zhakkar, *Daniil Kharms i konets russkogo avangarda* (St. Petersburg, 1995), 20. There is also Samuel Beckett who, in a letter of 29 December 1957 to Alan Schneider, wrote of his work on *Endgame* saying that it was a simple selection of basic tones and sounds expressed as fully as possible.

5   Claude Bonnefoy, *Conversations with Eugene Ionesco* (New York: Holt, Rinehart and Winston, 1970), 121.

6   For Kruchenykh's influence on Kharms see Zhakkar, *Daniil Kharms* [4].

7   A. Kruchenykh, *Pamiat' teper' mnogoe razvorachivaet: Iz literaturnogo naslediia Kruchenykh,* edited by Nina Gurianova (Berkeley: Berkeley Slavic Specialities, 1999), 205.

8   Compare this with Kruchenykh's revelations on *zaum*: 'A riddle… a reader is first of all curious and certain that the *zaum* means something, i.e., has some logical sense. So in a way the reader is hooked by the worm of the riddle or secret. Women and art have to have a secret. Saying 'I love' makes

a link – a very definite one – and people never want that. They are secretive, greedy, makers of secrets. So instead, 'I love' is written as something else equivalent and perhaps special: 'lefante chiol' or 'raz faz gaz... kho-bo-mo-cho-ro = gloom, and nihil, and modern art! As to whether the artist is deliberately hiding in the heart of *zaum* – I don't know.' (A. Kruchenykh, *Pamiat' teper' mnogoe razvorachivaet,* Nina Gurianova, editor [7], 201-2.)

9   Article by S. Patraskin, 'Bayachi budetliane' ['The Futurist Bards'], *Den'*, 8 December 1913. A similar interview of 1 December 1913 is found in Volume 1.

10   Vasily Kandinsky, 'On the Question of Form', *The Blaue Reiter Almanac* (1912), edited by Wassily Kandinsky and Franz Marc, 158. English translation edited by Klaus Lankheit (London: Thames and Hudson, 1974).

11   See Maurice Blanchot, 'Reflections on Nihilism: Crossing the Line', in *Friedrich Nietzsche,* ed. Harold Bloom (New York: Chelsea House Publishers, 1987), 37.

12   N. Evreinov, *Teatr kak takovoi,* 2nd edition (Berlin, 1923), 88.

13   A. Kruchenykh, *Vosropshchem / Let's Grumble* (St. Petersburg, 1913), 3.

14   See Evreinov, *Teatr kak takovoi* [12], 17, 34.

15   See I. Petrovskaia, *Teatr i zritel' rossiiskikh stolits 1895-1917* (Leningrad, 1990), 100-101.

16   See Kruchenykh's essay on opera, in A. Kruchenykh, *Pamiat' teper' mnogoe razvorachivaet,* Nina Gurianova, editor [7].

17   Cf. the proclamation in *Explodity / Vzorval*: 'Because of a base contempt for women and children in our language there will be only masculine gender'.

18   See M. Matiushin, 'Russkii kubofuturizm: Otryvok iz neizdannoi knigi *Tvorcheskii put' khudozhnika'*, *Nashe nasledie* 2 (1989), 133.

19   Antonin Artaud, *Selected Writings*, edited by Susan Sontag (Berkeley: University of California Press, 1988), 243.

20   Many scholars recently have identified this tendency in early Russian Futurism. Jean-Phillipe Jaccard, for example, considers it to be one of Futurism's principal themes: 'It is the principle of denial, which all too often serves to characterize Kruchenykh's art, that is the main error in appraisal of this poet, who is very difficult to academicize. On the contrary, in his poetics, as in the poetics of everyone who to any degree belongs to his tradition and in particular in that of Kharms, it is the idea of creation that dominates'. (Zh.-F. Zhakkar, *Daniil Kharms i konets russkogo avangarda* [4], 22).

21   See, for example, Artaud's 'Theatre of Cruelty: First Manifesto' (1932), in Antonin Artaud, *Selected Writings* [19], 243.

22   On language in the theatre of the absurd see Martin Esslin, *The Theater of the Absurd* (New York: Vintage Books, 2001), 339-349. ' "Absurd" originally means "out of harmony", in a musical context' according to Esslin, page 23.

23   By the dehumanization of art here is meant the notion developed by Heidegger
        in his 'Letter on Humanism', where ' ...the opposition to "humanism" in
        no way implies a defense of the inhuman but rather opens other vistas.... .
        To think against values is not to maintain that everything interpreted as a
        "value" – "culture", "art", "science", "human dignity", "world", and "God"
        – is valueless. Rather, it is important finally to realize that precisely through
        the characterization of something as "a value" what is so valued is robbed of
        its worth. That is to say, by the assessment of something as a value what is
        valued is admitted only as an object for man's estimation.... Every valuing,
        even where it values positively, is a subjectivizing. It doesn't let beings:
        be'. (250, 251) This rejection of humanism is justified on the grounds that
        placing humanity and its emotional, psychological, and social experiences at
        the center of the universe diminishes human spiritual potential – the essence
        latent not in humanity but in Being. Dehumanization does not at all mean
        resorting directly to abstraction, although an element of this is often present.
        Instead, the notion absorbed the essence of the spiritual revolution in art
        that the Futurists accomplished early in the century against what Malevich
        called the 'green world of flesh and bone' and that immediately embodied
        Nietzsche's call to struggle against 'the human, all too human' worldview.
24   See Antonin Artaud, *Theater and its Double* (New York, 1958).
25   'Interviews with Beckett: Tom Driver in Columbia University Forum',
        in Lawrence Graver and Raymond Federman, eds., *Samuel Beckett: The
        Critical Heritage* (London: Routledge, 1979), 219.
26   André Breton defined Surrealism as 'a kind of absolute reality', or 'Psychic
        automatism in its pure state, by which one proposes to express... the actual
        functioning of thought... in the absence of any control exercised by reason,
        exempt from any aesthetic or moral concern'.
27   Hans-Georg Gadamer, *Truth and Method* (New York, 1975), 94. It seems to
        me that Gadamar's position is most consistent with the anarchic aesthetics
        of the early avant-garde, which was constructed on a conscious erasure of
        traditional boundaries in art. In that context, play theory can be considered
        from positions that are diametrically opposed, for example, not only to
        classical aesthetics but especially to Mikhail Bakhtin's as expressed in
        his critique of play theory and expressive aesthetics. See M. M. Bakhtin,
        Estetika sloveskogo tvorchestva (Moscow, 1979), 67-68.
28   A. Kruchenykh, *Vozropshchem* [13], 9.
29   Here it is appropriate to recall Jacques Lacan's hypothesis that the substance
        of the unconscious resembles in many respects the typological structure of
        language.

THE WORD

'In the discovery of words: the break away from the meaning of words – the right of a word to be independent, hence, new creations of words (discovery by the genius, Khlebnikov).'

Mikhail Matiushin, 'Futurism in St. Petersburg:
Performances on the 2nd, 3rd, 4th, and 5th of December 1913'
First Journal of Russian Futurists, January 1914

Aleksei Kruchenykh

NEW WAYS OF THE WORD
(A language of the future, death to Symbolism)

nobody would argue if one says that we have no literary critics (judges of speech-creation)

one cannot accept such vampires feeding on the blood of 'the mighty deceased', stranglers of the young and lively

vampires, grave-diggers, country bumpkins, parasites – these are the only names worthy of our critics

their perennial occupation, even desire!, is to gnaw at each others' throats, pecking, drowning 'in a spoonful of water'

our critics love to settle scores or engage in political or family investigations and they always leave the question of the *word* to one side

Russian readers (even they!) despise them and disgustedly push aside the cud proffered them in place of food

but to the disgrace of genuine connoisseurs and lovers of art, we have to add this – that the necessary word never has never been said

It is not surprising that these 'little critics' throw mud at *us*, the bards [*bayachees*] of the future

We have become like warriors who attacked in the dim morning the idle enemy – who now, for the fun of the victors and the whole world, kick each other, grab each others' hair, while the defeated can only throw back *mud* and *abuse*

we are not afraid of these warriors and their panic is our goal!

watch out, you fat-lipped ones!

we show the weapon cunningly sharpened and the best cast, the weapon that you lecherously wanted to seize but only managed to cut your hand with…

before us there was no art of the word

there were miserable attempts by slavish thought to recreate its beingness, philosophy and psychology (what used to be called novels, stories, poems, etc.) were little rhymes for domestic and family use, but the art of the word

didn't exist.

strange? we can say more: everything was done to muffle the original sense of the native language, to unhusk from the word the fruitful grain, castrate it and send it out into the world as a 'clear, clean, honest, sound Russian language', despite the fact that it was no longer a language but already a miserable eunuch, incapable of giving anything to the world. It is impossible to cure or perfect it and we were perfectly right to declare: 'Throw Pushkin, Tolstoy, Dostoyevsky and Co. overboard from the ship of modernity' [in *A Slap in the Face of Public Taste*] so that they don't foul the air! After the ballads and 'Song of Igor's Campaign', the art of the word was falling and in Pushkin's time it was even lower than in Tredyakovsky's time (although the 'lines of communication' were improving. See below.).

The clear and decisive evidence of the fact that up to now the word was shackled in its *subordination to thought.*

up to now it has been asserted:

'(The) thought dictates the rules to the word, and not the reverse.'

We pointed out this mistake and produced free, transrational and universal language.

Formerly, Artists faithful to the word went via the thought. We, however, go via the word to immediate comprehension.

In art, we now have the first experiments of the language of the future. Art marches in the avant-garde of psychic evolution.

At present, we have three units of psychic life: sensation, representation, concept (and idea), and a fourth is starting to be formed – 'higher intuition'. (*Tertium Organum* by Ouspensky)

In art we declared:

THE WORD IS WIDER THAN THE MEANING

the word (and its contents – sounds) is not only a bob-tailed thought, not only logic, but mainly transrational (the irrational parts, mystic, and aesthetic)...

gladiators and swordsmen
[*gladiatori y mechari*]

the thought is the same but the words are different, and inasmuch as I would rather say that, '*smekhiri*' ['laughers'] and '*mechari*' ['swordsmen'] have one meaning, rather than Swordsmen and Gladiators, because the sound content of the word lends to it a tinge [colouration] of life and the word can only be perceived, actively affect you, when it possesses this tinge gladiators – dim grey foreign. swordsmen – bright colourful and gives us a picture of mighty people armour-plated in copper and chain mail

in the stock exchange [*birzha*] and in Metzl's office[1] one has to make use of, like an abacus, the first word, which is as dead and colourless as a telegraph code, in art it is a dead man at a banquet

Lermontov has disfigured the Russian bard's chant (poetry), and brought in a stenching corpse, flaunting it around in *l'azur*[2]...

morgue – it's funny and reminiscent of a fat German full of beer, *'truparnia'*[3] – neologism of *corpserie* [corpse-repository] even gives the sensation of a mortuary

university – you can wind up dogs with this, compulsory Education convinced us of the importance of the referent, etc., etc.

Every letter is important, every sound!

Why should one borrow from the languageless 'Germans' [i.e., 'foreigners'] when we have our own splendid language?

Russian readers got used to castrated words and can even see in them those algebraic signs which accomplish mechanically the task of the little thoughts, while they do not notice all that is alive super-consciously in the word, everything that connects it with its sources, the sources of being.

Art can only deal with what is alive – it doesn't give a damn for the dead! And writers themselves were anguished – they themselves understood the uselessness of all that had been created.
'O, if only without words my soul could express itself.' (Fet).
'*Thought* spoken out is a lie.' (Tyutchev)

thrice correct!

Why couldn't one get away from the thought and write without using words – concepts, but with words freely formed?

If the artist is powerless it means he has not mastered his material!..

People of exceptional honesty – Russian sectarians – determined that:

Possessed by religious inspiration (inspiration is always exalted) started talking in the language of the Holy Spirit (in their own splendid expression), drank 'the living water' [as in Holy Water].

And so the *new* word came about which is no longer a lie but a real confession of belief, a 'revelation of things unseen'.

> 'namos pamos bagos
> gerezon drovolmirye zdruvul
> dremile cherezondro fordei'
> (from the speech of the flagellant Shishkov)

It is remarkable that some sectarians [*reclusniks*] from amongst the ordinary peasants suddenly started talking not only in this transrational language, but also in *many foreign languages hitherto unknown to them!*

So, passing those real prophets by, those explorers of language (and critics as well) let them go unnoticed!.. But don't think that we are just imitators of these recluses.

The artist discovers amazing colours on an old wall – they give him an impulse and he creates a work of art which is as far from nature as the White Sea from the Black!..

It is surprising, the senselessness of our writers who are chasing after *meaning*.

They, wishing to portray the unintelligible alogicality of life and its horror, or to portray the mystery of life, resort to the same (as always, as always!) 'clear, precise' general language

it's like feeding a starving man with cobblestones or trying to catch a re-ide [fish of carp family; Kruchenykh adds invented *re*] in a rotten net!

We were the first who said that to reflect what is new and the future one needs *completely new words and a new way of putting them together.*

This will be such a decisive novelty, this combination of words according to their own inner laws, and these laws reveal themselves to the speech-creator; and not by the rules of logic or grammar, as was done before us.

Contemporary painters discovered the secret that 1) movement gives rise to salience (new dimension) and vice versa that salience gives rise to movement

and 2) incorrect perspective gives a new 4th dimension (essence of cubism).

Modern bard*s* have discovered: that incorrect sentence construction (in terms of logic and word formation) gives *movement and new perception of the world* and vice versa – movement and psychic change give rise to strange 'meaningless' combinations of words and letters.

For this reason we shook loose grammar and syntax; we found out that for the portrayal of dizzy-making modern life – and even more for the rapid life of the future – there is a need to combine words in a new way, and the more chaos we bring into the construction of sentences the better.

Sleek symbolists fear dreadfully that the public (of *Ogoniok / Small Light*, and *Russkaia Mysl / Russian Thought)* will not understand them. We are very pleased about this! All these narrow-minded Symbolists are afraid of how not to say the stupidity of meaninglessness (from the point of view of those same readers).

It is a well known fact that preppies try very hard to be intelligent and grown up!..

Even Dostoevsky remarked, 'Every writer has his own style and consequently also his own orthography.' But he himself only encroached on the area of the comma and the soft sign!..

> I suddenly thought: if I turn
> Upside down chairs and divans
> somersaulted clocks?...
> a new time would have started
> new countries discovered,
> And here in the room would be hidden
> the end of the tangle of things,
> faded by unkind yesterday-day
> the order of days.
> He was right next to me in the room!
> I suddenly believed that it was so
> and there is nothing to be afraid of
> but I had to find the secret sign.
>   'Barrel Organ' ['Sharmanka', 1909], Elena Guro

Incorrectness in the constructions of speech are possible:
1) incorrectness is unexpectedness is grammar
   a) a lack of agreement of case, number, tense and gender of subject and predicate attributes and those attributed: white-flying-passed by-lake
   b) the dropping of the subject or other parts of speech. dropping pronouns and prepositions, etc.
   c) arbitrary word-innovation (pure neologism):
      everything was to him *tirko* [invented sense of 'bad']
      (*A Trap for Judges*): dyr bul shchyl etc..
   d) acoustic [phonetic] unexpectedness:
      euy, rlmktzhg... (*Let's Grumble*)

It would not be out of the way to point to the chaps who recently published in Target[4] also borrowed our speech, which contains sometimes only vowels or consonants, sometimes scattering of letters and words. They hide their footprints and refer to 1912 as the time when their imitations were written (?!)! (Very original!)

e) unexpected word-formation: Khlebnikov

> Those who alarmed at midnight and saddener
> Call sobbingly pitied
> For having once whistled
> The lead is unleaded.
>
> Thunder boom, rocket blast, roar, racket?
> Then in that black embreak another deathling
> Falls face down, goes to ground,
> And gluts earth with rivulets of blood.
>
> 'These gather-goods are mine,' MOR says
> And fingers what was once a young man
> Who lies before him like a plowed field,
> Face down, fresh sown with seeds of lead.[5]
>
> (V. Khlebnikov, 'War-Death', *Union of Youth* 3)

Thanks to this unexpectedness an impression of war is almost deception of feelings.

Examples of neologism, see also E. Guro, *A Trap for Judges II*.

2) incorrectness of semantic order:

a) in the development of the action:

> I forgot to hang myself
> I fly to the Americas
> someone boarded a ship
> is he at least on the bow
>
> from *Explodity* (See also "Cockerel of Wisdom", *A Trap for Judges II*)

b) unexpectedness of comparisons:

> pokers sound like fires
>
> (*Worldbackwards*)

These do not exhaust all the examples using incorrectness and unexpectedness: (not by accident are they incorrect); for example one can have unusualness of metre, rhyme, inscription, colour and location of words, etc.

We aim only to point out the means of incorrectness and point out its necessity and importance for art.

We aim to underline the capital importance for art of all roughness, discordance (dissonance) and pure primal grossness.

When the puny and pale little man wanted to refresh his soul by contact with the strong rough gods of Africa, when he fell in love with their wild free language and the cutting animal sharpness of the eyesight of these primaeval men, then seven nannies instantly yelled and tried to protect the lost baby 'you are wallowing in cruelty and egotism' – shouts A. E. Redko (see *Russian Wealth*, July of this year). Your way is the abyss, slyly shouts Benois. Don't talk nonsense warns Briusov, and the others simply cackle, hiss and spit.

And everyone offers their advice, their weedy, bloodless philosophy without realising that it is only unsuccessful poetry (which was well known to past prophets!)...

Before us narration was boring and syrupy (3,000 pages!) which sickens the modern fast soul perceiving the world lively and spontaneously (intuitively) as if going into the things and phenomena, the transrational in me and of me, and not sitting somewhere on the side listening only to descriptions and narrations.

Our new methods teach us a new understanding of the world, breaking the squalid construction of Plato, Kant and other such 'Idealists' where man was not at the centre of the universe but behind the curtain.

Formerly the world of artists had two dimensions – length and width. Now it has gained depth and salience, movement and weight, a tinge [colouration] of time and so on and so on.

We have started to see *here* and *there*. The irrational [*zaumny*] is given to us as immediately as the rational [*oomy*].

We don't need a mediator of symbols, thoughts; we give our own new truth, and do not serve the reflection of some sun (or a log?).

The idea of Symbolism inevitably offers limitation to all creators and a truth hidden somewhere with an *honest uncle.*

Of course with this premise, where can you find the joy, spontaneity and conviction of creation? It is not surprising that our sour Symbolists are dying out and going to make money at the [newspapers] *Niva [The Cornfield]* and *The Small Light...*

We were the first to find the thread in the labyrinth and walk freely in it.

Symbolism does not stand up to the views of modern gnoseology and the honest soul. The more truth is subjective, the more it is objective. Subjective objectivity – that is our way. No need to be afraid of total freedom – if you don't believe in Man, don't have any truck with him!

We split the object open!

We started to see through the world.

We learnt to observe the world from the end, we are pleased with this reversed movement (as regards the word, we noticed that *we could read it backwards and then it gains an even deeper meaning!)*

We can change the weight of objects (the secular eternal *earth-gravitation)*, we see buildings suspended in the air and the weight of sounds.

In this way we give the world new content...

Creation is always inspired. God could be black and white, uneven and multiarmed – *he is mystery* but not *zero*, even if it were repeated a hundred times in a row.

The Italians playing at Futurists with their endless ra-ta-ta ra-ta-ta liken themselves to Maeterlinck's heroes, thinking that the door, repeated 100 times, turns into revelation.

These mechanical contrivances – soulless, monotonous – lead to the *death of life and art.*

It is not to wind up the reader with rustling emptiness and annoying barking, but it is in looking for ever new means appropriate to portraying the paths which cross and launch us, we who are in search of the future, into marshes and emptiness, we who choose *insidious* paths which confuse beginners because of their unexpected ups and downs. There can be discordance (dissonance) in art, but there must not be any cruelty, cynacism or impudence (from which the Italian futurists are profiting) – just as you cannot mix war and punch-ups with the creative work.

We are serious and solemn, and not destructively rude...

We have a high opinion of our Motherland!

Don't get carried away by foreign imitation.

Don't use foreign words in literary works; they are only appropriate in one instance – when you want to add a petty, insulting meaning to a word.

Remember: Pushkin, asked about the intelligence of the person with whom he had talked, replied: I don't know, we spoke in French!..

Create new native words!

New content *can only emerge* when new methods of expression and form have been achieved.

Once you have got a new form, it follows that you will have a new content. In this way, form determines content.

Once speech-creating is brought about by a *new deepening* of the spirit and throws new light on everything.

It is not the new things (objects) of creation that determine its true novelty.

New light, thrown onto an old world *can give the most whimsical play.*

Those who have no new light grab convulsively any new objects but their situation is made even sadder because 'new wine instantly rips through old flasks' – thus ended the vain efforts of Briusov-Verbitskaya, Balmont-the-eternal balalaika player, Sologub-the-cake, Andreev-the-retired and the ego 'futurist' yawners Severyanin, Ignatiev, Vasilisk Gnedov, etc.

I won't even mention Gorky, Kuprin and Chirikov and the other 'realists' or 'classics' whose works nobody reads.

Can one really compare those ugly little joys of previous lands with the joy of existence in the new dimensions?

Do not yield to the rebukes and 'good advice' of the cowardly little souls whose eyes are always looking backwards...

First published in *The Three / Troe*, September 1913, as 'Novye puti slova'.

Translated from the Russian by Christiana Bryan and S. I. Tverdoklebov. Use of upper and lower case, as well as punctuation and indentations, follow Kruchenykh's original.

Notes

1   This is a reference to the Ego-Futurists, whose leader, Ivan Ignatiev had an interest in the advertising agency, Metzl and Co.. Ed.
2   *Azur* in French is *blue* – as in the sky. Kruchenykh, in adding the soft sign, is piling mockery on mockery in the pretentious use of French words in Russian poetry and in the language of the Court. Ed.
3   Neologism from Khlebnikov's play in verse, *Marquise Dezès*. Ed.
4   That is, *Donkey's Tail and Target* of July 1913, in which the article by S. Khudakov (unidentified and thought to be a pseudonym of Ilya Zdanevich) strews letters across the page. Ed.
5   The last two verses translated by Paul Schmidt in Velimir Khlebnikov, *Selected Writings of the Futurian*, Harvard University Press, 1985.

Christopher Dempsey

ON *ZAUM* AND ITS USE IN
VICTORY OVER THE SUN

In 'Declaration of Futurism', F. T. Marinetti proclaims that 'the essential elements of our poetry will be courage, audacity and revolt', that the Futurists 'intend to glorify the love of danger, the custom of energy, the strength of daring', and that they 'wish to exalt the aggressive movement, the feverish insomnia, running, the perilous leap, the cuff and the blow'.[1] In *A Slap in the Face of Public Taste*, the Russians state that, '*We* alone are the *face* of *our* Time', that they intend to 'Throw Pushkin, Dostoevsky, Tolstoy, etc., etc., overboard from the Ship of Modernity', while they '*order* that the poets' *rights* be revered'.[2]

These basic tenets of Futurism applied to both the Russian and Italian models, but the Russian idea of a language that transcended rational thought, called *zaum* (pronounced zah-oom), differentiated the two models. Succinctly, *zaum* is a neologism, coined by Kruchenykh, that describes words or language possessing indeterminate meaning. Usually the term is rendered as 'transrational', 'transreason', or 'trans-sense', though other translations are not uncommon.

Zaum is a difficult idea to understand because the Futurists used it inconsistently, defined the concept in contradictory terms, and often wrapped their explanations in incredulous rhetoric. Ultimately, there is a significant difference between the Futurists' conceptualisation of *zaum* and their application of it, and several studies have attempted to reconcile these differences.[3] Rather than following these studies towards an explanation of *zaum*, this essay only provides some background on the genesis and development of the term, as well as an illustration of some of the difficulties in its definition, by looking at some of the manifestos that discuss the concept and examining specific instances of its use in *Victory Over the Sun*.

The notion of *zaum* developed over a two-year period during 1912 and 1913. As is often the case, practice preceded a theoretical description, which in turn preceded a theoretical name.

The earliest use of *zaum* appears in Kruchenykh's poem 'Dyr bul shchyl' from his book *Pomade*, which appeared at the beginning of 1913. The five-line poem consisted entirely of indefinite words:

Dyr bul shchyl
  ubeshchur
    skum
  vy so bu
  r l ez[4]

Kruchenykh preceded the poem with a paragraph describing the poem as written 'in their [*sic*] own language' with words '[without] a definite meaning'.[5] The foundation of this new language appears in the first two rights of poets, listed in the first manifesto of the Russian Futurists, *A Slap in the Face of Public Taste*, of December 1912 (officially published in January 1913):

1.   To enlarge the scope of the poet's vocabulary with arbitrary and derivative words (Word-novelty).
2.   To feel an insurmountable hatred for the language existing before their time.[6]

Interestingly, it was not Kruchenykh who began the process toward *zaum*. Instead, David Burliuk, a founding member of Hylaea and the editor of *A Slap in the Face of Public Taste*, suggested to Kruchenykh at the end of 1912 that he 'write a whole poem of "unknown words",' the result being 'Dyr bul shchyl'.[7]

In the spring of 1913, Kruchenykh first attempted to codify the theories of *zaum* in the pamphlet, *Declaration of the Word as Such*. It is here that he first uses the term, albeit in adjectival form, 'transrational language' (*zaumniy yazik*), in the opening point of eight presented in the order 4-5-2-3-1-6-7-8, which describe the new language. Here, Kruchenykh states that an artist should be free to express himself not only in the common language, but also in a personal one, and one that has no definite meaning, a transrational language. In four other points, Kruchenykh uses words that indicate he perceived *zaum* as an interaction between speaker and listener instead of writer and reader:

5.   ... The lily is beautiful, but the word 'lily' *(lilia)* has been soiled and 'raped'. Therefore, I call the lily, 'euy' – the original purity is re-established... .

2.   consonants render everyday reality, nationality, weight – vowels, the opposite: A UNIVERSAL LANGUAGE... .

3.   a verse presents (unconsciously) several series of vowels and consonants. THESE SERIES CANNOT BE ALTERED. It is better to replace a word with one close in sound than with one close in meaning (bastcast-ghast)... .

7.   In art, there may be unresolved dissonances – 'unpleasant to the ear' – because there is dissonance in our soul by which the former are resolved... .[8]

Kruchenykh's focus on how words sound and are subsequently perceived indicate that he thought of *zaum* as an oral phenomenon. Replacing words close in sound instead of meaning alludes to this reading, as does his discussion of 'unresolved dissonances'. The remaining two are not as clear, but they seem to imply language as it is spoken, not read.

The most detailed explanation of *zaum* appears in his manifesto, 'New Ways of the Word' (in this Volume). Here, Kruchenykh divides *zaum* into two categories – grammatical irregularity and semantic irregularity – that are further divided into sub-categories, of which most have an example from earlier works by Kruchenykh, Khlebnikov, or Guro.

Grammatical irregularity has five sub-categories: (1) the lack of agreement in case, number, tense, or gender between subject and predicate or adjective and noun; (2) elimination of the subject or other parts of speech like pronouns or prepositions; (3) arbitrary word-novelty, or pure neologism, for which he provides 'Dyr bul shchyl' as one example and refers the reader to *A Trap for Judges II* (*Sadok Sudei II*) for others by Guro; (4) unexpected phonetic combination, for which he gives '*euy, rlmktzhg*' from his *Let's Grumble* of 1913; and (5) unexpected word formation, which has a rather lengthy example from Khlebnikov's poem 'War-Death' published in *Union of Youth* 3.[9]

The second category, semantic irregularity, has two sub-categories, each provided with an example from Kruchenykh's earlier works. The first of these sub-categories, semantic irregularity in plot development, has no explanation, but only an example from *Explodity*:

I forgot to hang myself
I fly to the Americas
          someone boarded a ship
is he at least on the bow.

The second sub-category, unexpected simile, also lacks any explanation, but has an example from *Worldbackwards*:

pokers sound like fires[.]

Despite being Kruchenykh's most thorough attempt to explain *zaum* through classification, the description in 'New Ways of the Word' is full of contradictions and inconsistencies that make modern day analysis problematic. Although *zaum* represented a transrational language, Kruchenykh based his categories on rational language.

Furthermore, Kruchenykh's assertion that these categories did not exhaust all possible forms of *zaum* raises additional questions as to exactly how much the language could encompass or, in practical terms, at what point does *zaum* simply become bad spelling, bad grammar, or nonsense, and vice versa. Even the categories that Kruchenykh lists create a canvas that is much too broad, for on the one hand, the focus is on individual words – neologisms, non-agreeing words, eliminated words – while on the other hand, the focus is on the larger concepts of phrases and plot. Kruchenykh wants to take disparate concepts and put them under the single umbrella of *zaum*, but in doing so he weakens his explanation. These problems appear not only in this manifesto, but also in the others about *zaum*, and this is the reason why scholars rely heavily on the literary works of the Futurists to explain the concept.

Literary scholars have often looked at *Victory Over the Sun* because it was the largest work to date that had used *zaum*, although it does not use it exclusively.[10] Instead, it juxtaposes *zaum* with rational language throughout the entire work.

The main idea of the opera is the conquest of the sun to usher in a new era of Futurism, but the story is dominated by seemingly random events. It begins with a Prologue by Khlebnikov that has very little to do with the rest of the opera, and even focuses on different aspects of *zaum* than Kruchenykh's text, which is concerned almost exclusively with grammatical irregularities including verbs as nouns and vice versa, incorrect word gender, and words in the wrong grammatical case; and single words formed from the linking of several.

The plot of the opera seems to make little sense, as it falls under the category of semantic irregularity. The first event of the opening act is the tearing of the curtain by two Strongmen. They speak of the future and tell of plans to capture the sun and confine it. As they leave, a figure representing Nero and Caligula as one person enters and is met by the Traveller Through

All Centuries, and they both argue about the past and future. As the Traveller explains that he had come from the 35th century, the Certain Person with Bad Intentions enters and shoots at the Traveller with a rifle, but misses. The Traveller leaves as the Bully enters and sings a song. The Certain Person with Bad Intentions attacks the Bully as the scene ends. The second scene begins with Enemy soldiers in Turkish costumes. One of the soldiers gives flowers to the Certain Person with Bad Intentions, who tramples on them and then begins fighting with himself. As this occurs, Sportsmen and Strongmen enter and they again talk about the future and their plans. The scene ends as both Strongmen sing about the conquest of the sun. The third scene consists only of Funerarians – Kruchenykh's neologism – who sing the following song. The lyrics have a certain lack of logical coherency typical in the rest of the text of the opera:

> To smash the turtle
> To fall on the cradle
> Bloodthirsty turnip's
> Greet the cage
>
> The fat bedbug smells of the coffin…
> A little black foot …
> The squashed coffin rocks
> A lace of shavings curls.

The fourth scene begins with someone talking on the telephone who has just been informed that the sun has been captured. A group then walks in carrying the sun, but it cannot be seen because the group is crowded closely together. They sing about the future after the victory over the sun as the act ends.

The second act begins in the future in a place called the Tenth Land. The "Mottled Eye" enters and states that the remnants of the past are leaving. As he says 'and the skull like a bench has galloped into the door', he runs away. Next, the New enter from one side of the stage while the Cowards enter from the other. The New speak of the new lightness of air in this Future and indicate that those who could not adapt tried to drown or went mad. Next, the Reader enters, and as he describes the wonders of life without a past, the Fat Man enters, in a state of confusion. He had been sleeping and cannot find the sunset. As he tries to hide, the Reader quickly tells the Fat Man about all that has happened and the beauty of the new world. The Fat Man cannot cope with these changes as the scene ends. The final scene begins with the Fat Man, still confused, looking for a way out of the Tenth Land. He meets the Old Resident, who shows him an entrance that will take him back, but the Fat Man is scared and does not take it. As an Attentive Workman and Sportsmen enter, they sing about the Tenth Land. Suddenly, a plane crashes on stage and the Aviator emerges unharmed and sings an army song. The Strongmen enter and conclude the opera with an echo of the opening lines, 'the world will perish but to us there is no end!'.

Symbolic representations occur quite frequently in *Victory Over the Sun*. The principal figure, the Sun, acts as an all-encompassing representation of Symbolist ideas whose conquest signals the rise of a new literary age. The remaining characters often act as symbolic representations rather than developmental figures. The Strongmen, Nero and Caligula as one person, the Fat Man, the New, Sportsmen, the Certain Person with Bad Intentions, the Reader, the Traveller, and the Aviator all appear in at most a few scenes, disappearing after exposing their traits. All the positive aspects of these personalities are associated with the Tenth Land, while the negative aspects remain attached to the old world:

> The old culture has its patrons (Nero and Caligula), its self-obsessions (the sun, the Ill-Intentioned One) and its dead weight (skulls as benches, a Fat Man, etc.). The new culture is strong (Strong Men), agile (Sportsmen), can speak with a fresh clarity (the Elocutionist), and above all flies to new regions and is represented by the Time Traveler and the Aviator and their respective machines.[11]

Scholars have seen references to Symbolist ideas and drama in *Victory Over the Sun*, including works by the Symbolists Aleksandr Blok and Valeri Briusov.[12] The connection to Symbolist ideas is interesting because the Futurists harshly criticised the Symbolists in several of their manifestos, including *A Slap in the Face of Public Taste*, *The Word as Such*, and 'New Ways of the Word'. In the latter essay, Kruchenykh criticises the Symbolists for their lack of creativity and dullness:

> Sleek symbolists fear dreadfully that the public (of *Ogoniok / Small Light*, and *Russkaia Mysl / Russian Thought*) will not understand them. We are very pleased about this! All these narrow-minded Symbolists are afraid of how not to say the stupidity of meaninglessness (from the point of view of those same readers).

Kruchenykh continues his attack by pointing out the differences between the Symbolists and the Futurists:

> We don't need a mediator of symbols, thoughts; we give our own new truth, and do not serve the reflection of some sun (or a log?).

Kruchenykh's public attacks against the Symbolists, while simultaneously adapting their ideas for his own purpose, is another example of Futurist sabre rattling and practice moving in opposite directions from each other. Kruchenykh wants to be independent of the previous literary movements but cannot seem to escape their influences, just as the Russian Futurists can't escape the influence of the Italians.

Throughout the libretto Kruchenykh uses grammatical irregularities as well as neologisms and unexpected phonetic combinations. Two songs, one in vowels and the other solely in consonants (Scene 6), use the ideas of unexpected phonetic combinations and neologism.[13] These are the 'lyrics' to the song of consonants:

```
        l   l   l
        kr      kr
         tlp
         tlmt
        kr  vd  t   r
         kr  vubr
         du      du
        ra          l
          k  b  i

              zhr

    vida

        diba
```

Scholars have noted the recurring *kr* in this song, which may refer to Kruchenykh, and it also appears on Malevich's design for the opening scene's curtain.[14] Others have indicated that these lyrics mimic the sounds of machines.[15] Other words are formed through combinations of letters that ordinarily don't occur together in Russian such as 'tlp' or 'zhr.' In addition, the phonetic similarities between the neologisms 'vida' and 'diba' and the palindromic properties of the line 'dr dr rd rd' appearing in the song of vowels also fall into the category of *zaum*. Kruchenykh wanted the actors to express each syllable between pauses in order to detach the sounds from the words in an attempt to detach the words from their meaning. One of the actors, K. Tomashevsky, also commented on this technique in his recollections:

> The situation was much worse with Kruchenykh's 'opera'. Kruchenykh asked us to pronounce all the words with pauses between each syllable. It sounded like: 'The cam-el-like fac-to-ries al-read-y threat-en us.'. As a matter of fact, he was constantly inventing and finding something new, and getting on everyone's nerves. He especially annoyed Rappaport, who was helping him direct the play.[16]

Other examples of *zaum* include the juxtaposition of words in the same sentence for purely sound value, such as *'samovar'* and *'samolyot'* (airplane) from the fifth scene and *'sarcha'* (a neologism or an eliminated syllable) and *'sarancha'* ([lo]cust) in the Bully's Song from the first scene. In this latter example, the word *sarcha* seems to be a favourite of Kruchenykh as it also occurs in 'Mutiny on the Snow', which was published in *A Trap for Judges II (Sadok Sudei II)* earlier in 1913.

The basic examples of *zaum* illustrated here are but a handful of those found throughout *Victory Over the Sun*. As the first large-scale endeavour by the Futurists to apply the theories in 'New Ways of the Word' to a dramatic work, *Victory Over the Sun* holds a vital place in the development of Futurist thought. Yet it is important to realise that while this work represents the culmination of Kruchenykh's ideas published during these two years, it still was a point along a longer journey. Kruchenykh would continue to refine his theories regarding *zaum* for many years after *Victory Over the Sun*.

Notes

1   F. T. Marinetti, 'Declaration of Futurism'. Facsimile of his own English translation in Jean-Pierre Andreoli-de-Villers, *Le Premier Manifeste du Futurisme: Edition Critique avec, en Facsimilé, le Manuscrit original de F. T. Marinetti* (Ottawa: Editions de L'Université d'Ottawa, 1986), 126-127.

2   Anna Lawton and Herbert Eagle, eds., *Russian Futurism through Its Manifestoes, 1912 – 1928* (Ithaca: Cornell University Press, 1988), 51.

3   See E. K. Beaujour, 'Zaum', *Dada/Surrealism* 2 (1972), 13-18; Gerald Janecek, 'A *Zaum* Classification', *Canadian-American Slavic Studies* 20 (1986), 37-54; Gerald Janecek, *Zaum: The Transrational Poetry of Russian*

Futurism (San Diego: San Diego State University Press, 1996); Lawton and Eagle [2], 12-20; Vladimir Markov, *Russian Futurism: A History* (Berkeley: University of California Press, 1968); Viktor Shklovsky, 'On Poetry and Trans-Sense Language', translated and annotated by G. Janecek and P. Mayer, *October* 34 (1985), 3-24; et al.

4   Facsimile in Russian reproduced in Janecek, *Zaum*, Ibid., 54.

5   Ibid., 54.

6   Lawton and Eagle [2], 51-52.

7   Janecek, *Zaum* [3], 49.

8   Lawton and Eagle [2], 67-68.

9   Kruchenykh, 'Novye puti slova', in *Troe* (St. Petersburg: Zhuravl', 1913), 30-31. In English translation as 'New Ways of the Word', the preceding article in this volume.

10   See John E. Bowlt, 'The "Union of Youth"', in *Russian Modernism: Culture and the Avant-Garde, 1900 – 1930,* edited by G. Gibian and H. W. Tjalsma (Ithaca: Cornell University Press, 1976), 165-187; Charlotte Douglas, 'Birth of a "Royal Infant": Malevich and "Victory over the Sun"', in *Art in America* 62 (1974), 45-51; Gisela Erbslöh, *'Pobeda nad solnstem': Ein futuristisches Drama von A. Kruchenykh* (Munich: Verlag Otto Sagner, 1976); Janecek, *Zaum* [3]; Robert Leach, 'A Good Beginning: *Victory over the Sun* and *Vladimir Mayakovsky, A Tragedy* Reassessed', *Russian Literature* 13 (1983), 101-116; Christine Scholle, 'Krutschonykh – Sieg über die Sonne', *Das russische Drama*, edited by Bodo Zelinsky (Düsseldorf: Bagel, 1986), 239-251; et al.

11   Leach [10], 105. The names of the characters are the author's translations.

12   See Leach [10]; N. I. Khardzhiev, 'Polemchnoe imya', *Pamir* 2 (1987), 163-169; Jean-Claude Marcadé, 'Post-Face. La Victoire sur le Soleil, ou le merveilleux futuriste comme nouvelle sensibilité', *La victoire sur le soleil: Opéra* (Lausanne: L'Age d'Homme, 1976), 65-97.

13   The descriptions are Kruchenykh's: 'What particularly struck the audience were the songs of the Frightened One (in vowels) and the Aviator (solely consonants) — professional actors sang. The public demanded an encore, but the actors were timid and did not come out'. Kruchenykh, *Nash Vikhod*, p. 71; from the English translation in Volume 1 of this collection, "The First Futurist Shows in the World". A more accurate description would be 'mostly' vowels and consonants, respectively.

14   Erbslöh [10], 57.

15   Christine Scholle, 'Futurisches Theater. Majakovskij – Krucenych – Chlebnikov', in *Zeitschrift für Ästhetik und allgemeine Kunstwissenschaft* 27 (1982), 185.

16   K. Tomashevsky, 'Vladimir Mayakovsky', *Teatr* 4 (1938), 137-150. English translation in Ewa Bartos and Victoria Nes Kirby, 'Victory over the Sun', *The Drama Review* 15 (1971), 94-101, quotation on page 96.

ENTER THE PERFORMANCE

'They presented a new creation, free of old conventional experiences and complete in itself, using seemingly senseless words – picture-sound – new indications of the future that lead into eternity and give a joyful feeling of strength to those who reverently will lend an ear and look at it. They will light up with the joy of someone who has found a treasure and will not become a savage who laughs heartily – or becomes senselessly angry and animalistically spiteful when, for the first time, he hears or sees some complicated mechanism, invented after centuries of investigation, even something like the telegraph or liquid air.'

'There was such inner strength in each word, the scenery and Future Man appeared so powerfully and threateningly in a way never seen anywhere before, the music moved so gently and resiliently around the words, the paintings and Future People and Strong Men conquered the cheap, pretentious sun and lit their own light inside themselves.'

Mikhail Matiushin, 'Futurism in St. Petersburg: Performances on the 2nd, 3rd, 4th and 5th of December 1913', *First Journal of Russian Futurists*, January 1914

Caroline Wallis and Patricia Railing

JOURNEY IN SPACE-TIME
IN
THE VEHICLE OF DESTINY

The Cube and the Stage

'Welcome to the playhouse, the cube of your minds!', the Prologist might have said. For *Victory Over the Sun* is an action performed on a box-like stage and presents pictures of the liquid, moving thought-forms of our everyday minds. We are looking, glancing, and peering into the different dimensions of our mental spaces, past, present and future. In our minds we can go anywhere in time, anywhere in space, we can turn things upside down and we can look at them as if in a mirror, or through a glass darkly. Our mind is our world.

The stage on which *Victory Over the Sun* is played is inside of a box, a cube; it is a space parallel to the mind. The backdrops by Kazimir Malevich turn our minds around in images, while the words and music activate other senses.

Each of the six backdrops is a view of one of the six sides in the cube and presented in rotation. There are only six views, but each of them has been rotated at 90 or 180 degrees, turned upside down or inside out, or mirrored. Every face of the cube/stage/mind presents a different facet of reality because we see it from a different place and position in space. And so the mind revolves as we turn imaginatively in time and space.

This extreme movement of time and space of which the mind is capable was inspired initially by Parisian Cubist painting. Aleksei Kruchenykh, Mikhail Matiushin and Kazimir Malevich knew it well from the many works in the Moscow collection of Sergei Shchukin, and from Gleizes and Metzinger's late 1912 treatise, *On "Cubism"*, translated into Russian in early 1913. Not only were Russian painters influenced by Cubism, but so too were poets and composers, and Matiushin summed this up in his early 1914 review of the December 1913 St. Petersburg performance of *Victory Over the Sun*. There he wrote that 'what is happening in literature, music and the visual arts at the present time' is:

'In the visual arts: complete displacement of planes... by visual relationships... .

'In music: new ideas of harmony and of melody, new pitch (quarter of a tone), simultaneous movement of four completely independent voices....

'In the discovery of words: the break from the meaning of words – the right of a word to be independent, hence, new creations of words (discovery by the genius, Khlebnikov).' [1]

All that was new in these arts derived initially from Cubist creative principles and new ways of perception, and they were the inspirations for *Victory Over the Sun*.

A Collaboration

Although the Prologue was signed by Viktor Khlebnikov and the libretto was signed by Aleksei Kruchenykh, *Victory Over the Sun* is in many ways a collaboration between the two poets.

Kruchenykh's particular fascination was with 'the dizzy-making modern life – and even more the rapid life of the future', as he writes in 'New Ways of the Word', an article published in 1913 in *The Three,* in this Volume.[2] That is why he liked his word-pictures to be short and sharp, cut out of quick-shifting Cubist perception where we have to move in the word-images, expanding our imagination to the limit.

Khlebnikov's particular fascination was with the myth and folklore of ancient Slav traditions, and with number and calculations of time and human events over centuries. Kruchenykh incorporated aspects of these into his libretto.[3]

So *Victory Over the Sun* brings Slavic mythology and historical time-events together with cannon-balls and airplanes, it brings the inspiration of word-creation together with shifts of time and space. It brings farce and the absurd together with utter seriousness.

The two poets had written several articles together in 1912 and 1913, and this collaboration was almost necessary to their creativity. In many ways, then, *Victory Over the Sun* is the result of sharing between these two 'dream-magicians' and 'word-workers'. That is why in the discussion that follows on what *Victory Over the Sun* "is", mention is made just as frequently of one of the bards as of the other.

WHAT *VICTORY OVER THE SUN* IS

Victory Over the Sun is a tale about time.

We live our lives in time and are determined by that great regulator, the sun. Around midday we feel like a bit of lunch, and when the sun goes down we feel like a bit of supper. The time of day is determined by the sun, and so are we.

We count. We count the number of hours in a day and we count the number of years since we were born. We count the number of decades since, say, 1776 (American Declaration of Independence) and the number of centuries since 1066 (Battle of Hastings), the fall of Rome or the birth of Christ. Counting is time's measure.

Counting is not just in linear sequences but, as the spirit behind *Victory Over the Sun* demonstrated, time has patterns which can be discovered through numbers and articulations of numbers. Viktor – calling himself Velimir in 1913 – Khlebnikov came to be called the King of Time by his friends because the calculations in his Tables of Destiny reveal the past as well as the future, making it knowable.

Victory Over the Sun is a play about space.

We live our lives in space: in rooms, in houses, in gardens, in cities with their offices and sportsclubs and factories.

We know our spaces through the dimensions of space. A house is like a box: the front of the house is a plane of two dimensions, just as the sides and back are also. But front, back and sides together make three dimensions, and so we can go into the space of our house.

We move in space – forwards, backwards, to the right and left, up and down. And when we walk from the front door of our house into the living room we are walking in a direction, through space, and we are also walking through time. This is the fourth dimension – a body that moves in time in space: time is the fourth dimension of space.

So Victory Over the Sun is a window into the future and the victory over time conquered by number, and the victory over space conquered by time. *Victory Over the Sun* inaugurated the age of space-time in art.

Victory Over the Sun is a stroll through the sky.

On 6 April 1912 there was a partial eclipse of the sun which was seen over Russia. A full eclipse was predicted for 21 August 1914 and would be seen in the afternoon of that day. *Victory Over the Sun* took place between these two phenomenal celestial events. Perhaps the opera even intended – or pretended – to announce the coming eclipse as a 'prophecy'.

During a solar eclipse, the sun becomes invisible, day becomes dark, and for myth and legend, the sun is hidden, stollen, or dies. It is a time of fear – as the Strongmen in the opera say, 'The sun has hidden / Darkness has begun / Let us all take knives / And wait locked up'. (Scene 2)

When the sun re-emerges it is said to be a new sun, a transition from fear of the end to hope in the beginning, a new beginning. It is a time of rejoicing, and of change.

Victory Over the Sun is the victory of a new sun appearing after the death of the old sun. It is an allegory of new beginnings arising out of the demise of the old – an obvious reference to social and political orders, as well as a new state of awareness of space-time arising out of a new consciousness.

Victory Over the Sun is a shamanic voyage on the wings of an iron bird.

In his Prologue, Khlebnikov declares that the poet and author of the opera is a 'dreamcraftsman, a heaven-dweller and the doer of deeds'. Thus the charmed one, a magician of the word and a seer, charms us. The word is the magic which enables access to other realms.

For Khlebnikov, the word is power, a force *em*-powered by shamanism. As he wrote to Kruchenykh on 31 August 1913, 'For me, the important thing is to remember that the elements of poetry are elemental forces. They are an angry sun that strikes with a sword or a flyswatter at the waves of human beings. In general, lightning (the discharge itself) can strike in any direction, but in fact it strikes the point where two elements join. Such discharges sliced open the Russian language when it was centred on peasant-village life.'[4] This is what inspired him in the creation of neologisms from roots of words found in Slavic languages: his aim was to release their energy and discover their magic. He reduced the word to its basic units, as he did with number in his theory of time.

The magic of the word was also the source of discovery for Kruchenykh. For him, however, this discovery was focused on the then-modern world, the sensations of new technology and a future consciousness.

Victory Over the Sun brings the two worlds of past and future together. Through the transformative power of the word, the two bards exploded myth and modernity.

Now these four aspects of *Victory Over the Sun* will be discussed in more time and space detail.

Time

There are several kinds of time in *Victory Over the Sun*. There are linear time, simultaneous time, and reverse time.

Linear Time

In linear time events follow each other in chronological sequence. In the play, Nero and Caligula (united as one character) precede the arrival of the enemy troops in Turkish costume. That is, the two caesars of the Roman Empire – who were blood kin (uncle and nephew) and as one in the atrocities they committed – precede the Holy Roman Empire of Constantine, which was later defeated by the Muslim Turks. This Empire would be superceded by the Russian Empire of the tsars, czars (ce-czars). Linear time is rational time.

Simultaneous Time

When one is arriving by train at an airport and an airplane above is coming in for landing, these two separate events are taking place at the same time, simultaneously. For the observer this gives rise to a variety of experiences since the speed of the motion of the train and the plane are relative to each other and to the observer.

An example of simultaneous time in the play, and a juxtaposition, is found in the lines, 'An iron bird is flying / The wood goblin waggles his beard / Beneath the hoof of someone buried'. (Scene 2) These events are all spoken in the present tense so are apparently happening concurrently, simultaneously, even if in different locations and seemingly unconnected. In addition, Kruchenykh has joined imaginatively different events in space, linking simultaneous time with simultaneous space.

Reverse Time

After the capture of the sun in Scenes 5 and 6 there are parts where time seems to reverse, solar energy suspended behind the orb of the moon.

The Fat Man exclaims, 'how about winding up the clock. hey you stupid shaft where do you turn the clock? the hand?' To which the Attentive Workman replies, 'they both go backwards immediately before dinner.' So, of course, when will they eat, since dinnertime never comes!

And where will they have dinner? Since, continues the Fat Man, 'yesterday there was a telegraph pole here and there is a snackbar today, and tomorrow it will probably be bricks.' (Scene 6)

Khlebnikov had coined this very image in an undated letter to

Kruchenykh of 1913 writing, 'first people die, then they live and are born; at first they have grown-up children, then they get married and fall in love. I don't know whether you share this opinion, but for a Futurian, *The World in Reverse* [a collection published in December 1912] is like an idea suggested by life for someone with a sense of humour, since first of all the frequently comic aspect of the fates can never be understood unless you look at them from the way they end and, secondly, people so far have looked at them only from the way they begin. And so, take an absurd view of the difference between your desired ideal and things as they are, look at all things in terms of their return unto dust, and everything will be fine, I think.' [5]

The Fat Man nevertheless has regrets: 'where is the sunset?' he asks. And then discovers that he is in a new place in space: the 10th Land. There we find a new space and a new time, space-time.

SPACE

Just as there are several kinds of time in *Victory Over the Sun*, so there are also several kinds of space. These are determined by the six directions of three-dimensional space: forwards-backwards, right-left, up-down (or above-below). As each of these can also be reversed by turning them upside down, inside out, and in mirror reflection, we get a reverse perspective of objects in space.

The Six Directions of Space
We go forwards, we move backwards, we climb up steps and slide down slopes, we turn to the left or we turn to the right. These are the only directions in which we can move in space, and they can occur in succession, simultaneously, and in reverse.

Successive Space
Taking a step at a time up a flight of stairs is moving through space in succession. Indeed, there are steps that appear in Malevich's backdrops, reminding the viewer of this progression.

There are not many examples of successive space in the libretto, although one does find passages such as, 'There is much dust / Flood … Look / Everything has become masculine. / The he-lake is harder than iron'. (Scene 1) These sequences are apparently logically connected, but even if they are not, they follow each other, in succession, in this case from an event in space that resembles descriptions of volcanic eruptions: dust, flood, looking at it, a frozen lake of lava. It appears to be rational.

Simultaneous Space

If we imagine ourselves in the Luna Park Theatre in St. Petersburg in December 1913, we see people sitting in seats in the balconies, boxes and orchestra. This is simultaneous space. If we place Khlebnikov's imagery there then people are sitting in 'cloudbanks…, treetops…, and sandbanks…'. Just as the poet has put many incongruous images together in the reality of a theatre space, so a painter also puts many seemingly incongruous things together on a canvas, As Albert Gleizes and Jean Metzinger say in *On "Cubism"*, the artistic treatise enunciating these ideas for Cubism, a landscape in China and a landscape in France can appear together in a single painting.[6] A painter is free to juxtapose anywhere in space.

This device is exploited in the extreme in *Victory Over the Sun*, and there is no end to the number of examples that could be cited which are apparently logical or obviously non-logical, that is to say, transrational (*zaum*), beyond the rational intellect.

So there are: 'And cannon bodies! / We are toppling mountains!' (Scene 1), 'There is no more light of flowers / Skies cover yourselves with the rot' (Scene 2), 'from dragonflies / The lilies are drawn / by locomotive' (Scene 6), 'The people have come out onto the porch / Of the tea room waving [bathhouse] switches' (Scene 2).

Reverse Space

Turning space inside out, upside down, and reflecting as mirror images is one of the favourite amusements of Kruchenykh in the opera, and it is exploited masterfully in the backdrops by Malevich. Indeed, reverse space in its various guises is the key to reading what Khlebnikov called the painter's 'look-ats' in the Prologue.

Upside Down

Upside down space is an object turned 180° about the horizontal, so we can see something, or parts of it, in two ways: the right way up and upside down. 'Hey you take your feet off!' shouts the Fat Man as he 'leaves through the top window'. (Scene 6) For many things are upside down in the 10th Land. Later he says, 'all the paths have got mixed up and go up to the earth while there are no sideways… hey, if there is anybody of ours there, throw me some rope or say something…'. (Scene 6) The earth and sun have been turned upside down in their above-below relationship.

The backdrop for Scene 5 – where the square is divided on the diagonal and is half black (absence of light, darkness) and half white (presence of light) – is seen upside down, stage right of the backdrop for Scene 3. It has flipped in space, indicating that the cube itself has flipped over. There we witness the progression of the black over the white as the cube turns, the moon gradually covering the sun in the progression of the eclipse.

Inside Out

Everything is also inside out in the 10th Land. Like turning a glove, or a cube, inside out, in 'The 10th lands… the windows all face inside the house is fenced in…' says the Fat Man (Scene 6), and this can be seen on the backdrop.

Now that the sun has been captured by the moon and its light extinguished, One of the Many says, 'Our light is inside us / We are warmed by / The dead udder of the red dawn'. (Scene 4) This is a transposition of light from outside to inside, one's spiritual light replacing the light of the sun.

(The red rays of dawn are the earth's heat radiating outwards, those in the 10th Land now warmed by the earth instead of the sun. Sun and earth are again upside down in their usual relationship of above-below.)

Mirror Image

In mirror images there is a play between an object and its reflection: one is real and the other is an illusion. So the Fat Man says, 'gee, I can fall' then he 'looks at the section of the clock: the tower the sky the streets – all the tops facing downwards as if in a mirror'. (Scene 6)

Mirror images can be seen in Malevich's backdrops as, for example, in Scene 1 where the panel-like fluting (?) of the column or perhaps billowing veils (above) are in mirror image (below). There are also mirror images of three large steps at the bottom of Scene 2 which are reflected as two large steps turned at an angle at the top. These same steps are reversed by 90° in the backdrop for Scene 6.

The Converging of Time and Space

Parallels can be drawn between time and space from the above descriptions. Thus:

Linear Time and Successive Space are both the sequence of events in time and in space in which the connections are apparently rational and logical.

Simultaneous Time and Simultaneous Space are where unconnected events are taking place at the same time, or where unconnected objects can be seen all at once. This makes possible the juxtaposition of non-logical, irrational, or transrational relationships in *Victory Over the Sun*.

Reverse Time and Reverse Space are where time goes backwards and objects in space are not in their 'normal' or ordinary positions or relationships for the viewer. These provide much opportunity for transrational juxtapositions in the opera.

The Merging of Time and Space

For the poets, painter, and composer of *Victory Over the Sun*, the fourth dimension is movement *in* space and *as* time. Time is the fourth dimension of three dimensional objects in space.

Introducing the notion of dimension introduces thinking in terms of geometry, a point emphasised by P. D. Ouspensky in *Tertium Organum*, the book that had such an impact on Kruchenykh in the writing of *Victory Over the Sun*, as also on the painter and composer.

Since time is non-material, while objects are material, time and space belong to different geometries.

Objects, which are matter, exist in space in one, two, or three dimensions (i.e., line, plane, or cube/sphere/etc.), and this can be explained using Euclidean geometry, a geometry that corresponds to our logical, rational, and linear thinking.

Time, however, is non-matter, existing as states or properties of objects in movement; it can only be explained by non-Euclidean geometry. Even then, time as the fourth dimension of objects in space is elusive because it lacks classification in our logical, three-dimensional thinking. For the fourth dimension is non-logical, non-rational, and non-linear.

Having described the progression from one, to two, to three dimensions, each characterised in succession by extending in a direction outside of the space of the previous dimension, Ouspensky writes that '*By existing*, every three-dimensional body moves in time', where 'a four-dimensional body may be regarded as the trace of the movement in space of a three-dimensional body'. Hence every body, object, is a 'time-body' when it 'leaves the trace of its motion'. In fact, 'Four-dimensional space – time – is actually the distance between the forms, states and positions of one and the same body (and of different bodies, i.e. bodies which appear different to us). It separates those forms, states and positions from one another, and it also binds each one into some whole incomprehensible for us. This incomprehensible whole may be formed in time out of one physical body, or it may be formed out of *different bodies*.' [7]

In this context it might be said that *Victory Over the Sun* is a farce about the most unlikely juxtapositions of three-dimensional phenomena situated 'out of time'. Time, as the space occupied by the movement of things, is a logical and rational occurrence when a moving object leaves its trace – like the vapour trail behind an airplane. This 'time-body' coincides with our everyday experience.

Kruchenykh, on the other hand, uses the time-space relationship transrationally. 'The lilies are drawn / by locomotive' (Scene 6), 'the skull like a bench has galloped into the door.'. (Scene 5) *Victory Over the Sun* is shot through with these illogical, irrational relationships between time and space.

The logical part of the mind naturally matches like with like – the activity of the 'concrete' mind. So to challenge it with a torrent of unlikes during the performance is meant to force it to break away into another part of the mind – the imaginative, creative intelligence – in order to experience connections between apparently unconnected time and space.

So to encase the sun in a 'concrete' box reveals itself – think out of the box! Merging time and space irrationally is intended to expand our consciousness so that we un-learn our usual three-dimensional (or Marshall McLuan's one-dimensional) thinking and enter the world of four dimensional thinking, that of things + movement and time-awareness.

A STROLL THROUGH THE SKY

For common consciousness, whether primitive or modern, a solar eclipse is a sign and a signal of change. Known in advance only by calculations – whether a Stonehenge or the sophisticated calculations of astronomers – interpretations of a solar eclipse had relied on the readings and prophecies of the wise. This depends on understanding the laws of our planetary system, and it is only possible by a mind activity, by thinking. The cosmic mind and the human mind are linked.

In order to effect this, to understand its laws, we must expand our consciousness, we must become the wise. And to expand consciousness is one of the tasks of *Victory Over the Sun* – or as Ouspensky expresses it, to 'expand our apprehension'.[8] Using a cosmic event was sure to rivet the attention and make people sit up. For as the Fat Man says during the eclipse, 'such a pernicious climate even cabbages and leeks won't grow and the market – where is it then?'. (Scene 6) Without the sun there can be no life.

The New, however, welcome a new consciousness, a new life of the mind. 'It airs the whole city. It becomes easier to breathe for everybody', they say (Scene 6), now that they 'have shot into the past.' (Scene 5) They have rejected old forms of government, social structures, and hierarchies. They also relinquish all those hindering emotions that cause wars among nations and within oneself. 'One person brought his sadness saying, take it, I don't need it any more!' (Scene 5) And the Reader declares, 'how extraordinary life is without the past / With risk but without remorse and memories'. (Scene 5) Free from its determining tyranny and no longer judged by past values, the New can create new things because they are open to new ideas, new relationships, new time, new space, and a new sun. Above all, to a new and better world because they themselves are the creators of it.

There will even be a new language, necessary for expressing new sensations and new perceptions of a world with new inventions. Significantly, the Aviator's song is in a new language made up of consonants, the sounds and creative generators of all form.

The Aviator is also the geometer who represents the ascendance of mankind to the height of the clouds. The wings on Hermes' heels have become w-heels as the engine's roaring chariot traverses the skies. In space, floating, free from objects of orientation, the mind is liberated to experiment with geometry, articulating thought-forms in the mind. The experience is wonder, the concept is mental, and the action is thought, all driven by the power of the imagination. The form is not of our senses but is pure sensation, a mind thing. The Russians, it seems, may have been the first to get a man into space after all!

A SHAMANIC VOYAGE ON THE WINGS OF AN IRON BIRD

Velimir Khlebnikov was passionate about the indigenous and ancient culture of the Slavs. The Russian language had been 'infiltrated' by foreign words, especially French, the language of the tzars' court, since the 18th century, and that is why Khlebnikov's many neologisms devised for his Prologue replace the European origin of the words for 'theatre', 'stage', 'actors', 'tragedy', 'orchestra', etc., with words having Slavic roots.[9]

In his fascination with the folk customs, lore, and myth of the ancient Slavs, Khlebnikov found not only the roots of culture, but also their history. That is why references to the forces of nature in the elemental beings of the earth reveal ancient wisdom, just as the words themselves reveal the elemental forces of physics.

Thus in *Victory Over the Sun* we have water nymphs and a 'wood goblin' who 'waggles his beard / Beneath the hoof of someone buried' and 'violets moan'. (Scene 2)

But above all, *Victory Over the Sun* is the creation of a bard, that most ancient singer of tales. The poet is a 'dream-ruling song maker' and a 'dream craftsman', 'a magus' 'wearing wonderful drags, showing the morning and the evening in the acts' according to his own 'design', that of 'this heaven-dweller' 'and the doer of deeds', as Khlebnikov says in the Prologue. The poet, then, is a shaman, one who got his story during a flight to the middle space, the realm of the 'half-heavenly'. There is where inspiration can be found, there is where all time is visible, where the past and the future can be seen and expressed simultaneously – sometimes with the help of the transcendental powers of the mushroom, mentioned in the libretto!

In his memoirs, *Our Arrival*, of 1932, Kruchenykh writes that for all Khlebnikov's Slavophilia, he was forgetting that they were living in an urban and technological world. He says that Khlebnikov's 'profound interest in national folklore often served to obscure his perception of things modern.' [10]

So here is the urban bard-*cum*-aviator who travelled on the wings of an iron bird, the airplane. As the aviator crash-lands in the 10th Land he declares, 'I am alive only the wings are just a bit ruffled', then he sings a military song in a new language. (Scene 6) References abound in the mention of self-propelled driving machines like automobiles and airplanes, locomotives or steamengines, and other 'monsters with mottled eyes'; and there are also skyscrapers. The historical iron age of the cannon-ball has gone and the modern iron age is impelled, technology in the lead.

The ancient myth of elemental and celestial forces, which Khlebnikov transformed in the word and in his mathematics of physical forces in the universe, unites with the modern myth of the machine in what was their world of the future. It is our today.

BRIGHTLY SHINING SPOTS OF LIGHT

In *Tertium Organum* P. D. Ouspensky writes that the human mind 'has often been compared to a dark sleeping city in the midst of which watchmen's lanterns slowly move about, each throwing light on a small circle round itself. This is a perfectly true analogy. At each moment there come into focus a few of these circles illumined by the flickering light while the rest is plunged into darkness.

'Each small illumined circle represents an "I", living its own life, at times very brief. And the movement goes on endlessly, now fast, now slow, bringing out into the light more and more new objects, or else old ones from the realm of memory, or in torment going round and round the same persistent thoughts.

'This continuous movement which goes on in our mind, this constant shifting of light from one "I" to another, may perhaps explain the phenomenon of *motion* in the external visible world.'[11]

It may also explain the pictures in the playhouse created in words by Kruchenykh and Khlebnikov, under the roving coloured spotlights operated by Malevich, picking out now one performer then another, and sung in the shifting dissonant notes of Matiushin's score. *Victory Over the Sun* is about pictures, embodiments of thought-forms, arising and falling away in the vast space of our minds, but which we can now enjoy with our artistic senses inside the cube that is the stage.

Notes

1   Mikhail Matiushin, 'Futurism in St. Petersburg', *Futurists: First Journal of Russian Futurists*, No. 1-2, Moscow, 1914. Translated in Volume 1 of this collection.

2   Aleksei Kruchenykh, 'New Ways of the Word', *The Three*, St. Petersburg, 1913.

3   See Khlebnikov's articles published in *Slav*, his analyses of the letter and his Tables of Destiny in *Collected Works of Velimir Khlebnikov*, Vol. 1. *Letters and Theoretical Writings*, Paul Schmidt, translator, Charlotte Douglas, editor (Cambridge: Harvard University Press), 1987.

4   Ibid., 82.

5   Ibid., 74.

6   Albert Gleizes and Jean Metzinger, *On "Cubism"*, Paris, 1912, Chapter V. Translated into Russian as *O "Kubizm"* by Ekaterina Nizen and published in St. Petersburg in 1913. Nizen was the sister-in-law of Mikhail Matiushin

whose essay in *Union of Youth* 3, St. Petersburg, April, 1913, was a comparison of excerpts from it and P. D. Ouspensky's *Tertium Organum*.

7   P. D. Ouspensky, *Tertium Organum, The Third Canon of Thought, A Key to the Enigmas of the World*. Translated by Nicholas Bessaraboff and Claude Bragdon (London: Routledge & Kegan Paul, 1923 and 1981), 37-38. First published in St. Petersburg in 1911.

8   Ibid., 14.

9   See his various articles in *Collected Works of Velimir Khlebnikov,* Vol. 1. *Letters and Theoretical Writings* [3].

10   Aleksei Kruchenykh, *Our Arrival. From the History of Russian Futurism* (Moscow: RA, 1995), 49.

11   P. D. Ouspensky, *Tertium Organum* [7], 170-1.

THE SETS & COSTUMES

'In the visual arts: complete displacement of planes, displacements of visual relationships, introduction of new concepts of relief and weight, dynamics of form and colour.'

Mikhail Matiushin, 'Futurism in St. Petersburg: Performances on the 2nd, 3rd, 4th, and 5th of December 1913', *First Journal of Russian Futurists*, January 1914

New Man
(Private Collection)

Turkish Warrior
(Private Collection)

Strongman
(Private Collection)

John Milner

MALEVICH'S *VICTORY OVER THE SUN*

Shifting Sands and Literary Collaborations

Kazimir Malevich approached the collaborative project of *Victory Over the Sun* as a painter and printmaker. It was not his first collaboration. From 1910 to 1913 he had worked closely with the Futurist painters Mikhail Larionov and Natalia Goncharova, developing his peasant themes in response to Goncharova's peasant subjects and Larionov's soldier paintings. He shared their enthusiasm for the *lubok*, the popular print, non-European art, untaught artists' approaches, children's drawings and sign-painters' work, leading to anti-academic, 'neo-primitive' styles.

During the same period Malevich contributed illustrations to a whole suite of Futurist books by *Victory*'s librettist Aleksei Kruchenykh, his partner, the painter-printmaker Olga Rozanova (see her poster for *Victory Over the Sun* in Volume 1), and the composer-painter Mikhail Matiushin. All were keen supporters of the poet Velimir Khlebnikov. In this year of intense activity, Malevich began to shift his allegiance towards the most radical and innovative Futurist poets.

In Russian Futurist books painters responded to challenges set by their poet friends. Malevich's contributions sometimes have the look of incidental additions with more coherence among his graphic work as a whole than they achieve in the books themselves. His peasant imagery developed across several books to produce the anonymous, physically strong, female worker that is a uniquely Russian contribution to Futurism.

The small experimental books to which Malevich contributed also track his shifting allegiances in 1913. Kruchenykh's book *Explodity* (*Vzorval'*), published in June 1913, was illustrated by Goncharova, Malevich, and Rozanova. In the same month the poet published a second book, *Let's Grumble (Vozropshchem)*, this time illustrated by Malevich and Rozanova.[1] Malevich was shifting from the orbit of Larionov and Goncharova towards that of Kruchenykh and Rozanova. This was confirmed on the 18 – 19 July when Malevich joined Matiushin and Kruchenykh at Uusikirkko in Finland, where the ambitious Futurist opera was envisaged for production under the auspices of the Union of Youth in St. Petersburg, during its seventh exhibition (10 November 1913 to 10 January 1914).[2]

The first fruit of this 'All Russian Congress of Futurian Bards' (in Volume 1) at Uusikirkko was the book *The Three* (*Troe*), developed in a partnership that is recorded in a photograph of Matiushin, Malevich and Kruchenykh, wearing summer hats in a sunlit room at Matiushin's dacha (in Volume 1). The maquette of the publication that is visible in this photograph was almost complete, and already featured its neo-cuneiform lettering, layout and distinctive square format.[3] By September 1913 *Troe* was available and it included an excerpt from Matiushin's musical score of the opera. (In this Volume, p.108.)

Rehearsing *Victory*

Composer, poet and painter were collaborating closely together during the five months that led up to the opening of *Victory Over the Sun* in December. This gave Malevich detailed knowledge of the poetic and musical ideas of his Futurist colleagues, in particular the concept and practice of transrational '*zaum*' language of which the poets Khlebnikov and Kruchenykh were the pioneers. Malevich, who later wrote *zaum* verse, also immediately applied the term '*zaum* realism' to recent paintings. This collaborative team of poets Khlebnikov and Kruchenykh, and illustrators Malevich and Rozanova, created the founding texts that announced *zaum* in the book *The Word as Such* (*Slovo kak takovoe,* seen above with Malevich's lithograph *Reaper* on the cover). With Matiushin, they comprised the artistic production team of *Victory Over the Sun.*

In October 1913 David Burliuk planned his 'First Evening of Russian Futurist Word-Creators' to include Futurists from St. Petersburg and to promote their productions of *Victory Over the Sun* and *Vladimir Mayakovsky: A Tragedy.*[4] In December, *Expodity* was republished with additional illustrations by Nikolai Kulbin.

Malevich's illustrations in 1913 were of two kinds: lithographs of Futurist peasants; and dynamic urban subjects in which overlapping repeated forms track sequential movements. The latter includes the *Carriage in Motion*

published in *The Three* (in Volume 1).
The remarkable *Simultaneous Death of
a Man in an Airplane and on a Train,*
published in *Explodity* (illustrated right),
and the *Troe* lithograph, *The Pilot* (below,
right), were both produced in 1913. They
provide the closest imagery to *Victory
Over the Sun*, where the aviator is a key
figure, a Time-traveller, covered in slips

of paper bearing the dates of years, and crashing in
the final scenes of the opera, just as the Futurist poet
and pilot Vasily Kamensky crashed in actual life.

Malevich possessed the rare artistic ability
to move between contrasting subjects and styles
simultaneously, sometimes incorporating a multi-
plicity of styles and techniques into individual
canvases. In effect, he became a commentator on
the language of visual techniques as much in his
visual work as in his essays.

Victory Looms

During his work for *Victory Over the Sun,* Malevich continued his activities
as an illustrator of Futurist books, and as a Cubo-Futurist painter. He depicted
peasant imagery, mechanized movement (including flight), and *zaum.* There
was a further factor. Malevich's *Knifegrinder* (Yale University Art Gallery) of
1912 – 1913, with its scintillating light and repetitive mechanical movement,
was a painting suitable for an Italian Futurist exhibition. This depiction of
movement also interested Parisian Cubists including Fernand Léger and
Marcel Duchamp.[5]

Malevich was at his most prolific and diverse whilst developing
designs for *Victory Over the Sun*, a time when innovations in painting were
being launched all around him in Russia. He was particularly influenced by
Larionov's Rayism (Luchizm). His book entitled *Luchizm (Rayism)* had been
available since April 1913 with illustrations by Larionov and Goncharova.
Rayism acknowledged that the visible world is apprehended through light
entering the eye from an intense and energetic field of rays reflected from
everything visible. Rayism attempted to depict that field of energy, producing
a crystalline imagery of the intersecting rays by which the world is perceived.

It made for intensely dynamic paintings with barely recognizable imagery. This is the case in Malevich's *Pilot* lithograph. In *Victory Over the Sun* Malevich discovered the potential of coloured lights projected on stage, a far more dramatic and public arena in which to experiment with the ideas of Rayism while extending its techniques enormously. In the opera, Malevich's designs for backdrops have the format of paintings, but not Rayist paintings for they show no beams of light. They were, however, designed to receive rays of coloured light, which is why the designs remained black and white.

Levky Ivanovich Zheverzheev (1881 – 1942), the wealthy supporter of the Union of Youth and a prime mover in its theatrical projects, preserved many of the designs for *Victory Over the Sun*. His collection of theatre art,[6] hung on adjacent walls, displayed designs for three crucial productions: the 1911 production of *The Tale of Tsar Maksem'ian and his Disobedient Son Adolf,* designed by Vladimir Tatlin; the first productions of Futurist theatre, *Vladimir Mayakovsky: A Tragedy,* designed essentially by Josif Shkolnik with some cut-out characters painted by Pavel Filonov; and *Victory Over the Sun.* In this display, Zheverzheev featured the big red letterpress poster (in Volume 1) with its black central print by David Burliuk, surrounded by the set and costume designs by Malevich (see Dramatis Personae in Volume 1) all made on equal-sized paper. The set designs are executed in black, as are three of the costumes. The rest of the costumes are painted in water-colour.[7]

One additional set design is known from the libretto published by Matiushin and Kruchenykh. The design appeared on stage in a photograph published by the St. Petersburg newspaper, *Early Morning* (*Ranee Utro*), on 12 December 1913 (in Volume 1). There are six set designs for the six scenes. Even so there exist other working drawings and variants that Zheverzheev did not acquire, including a sequence of drawings of figures with playing card suits (spades, diamonds, clubs) for heads (below), one set in the State Russian Museum, St. Petersburg. The diamond-headed warrior carries a sabre and is inscribed 'Turkish Warrior' by Malevich (below centre). There is also a design for the New Man (below right) and a Strongman (left).

The set designs as a group were roughly executed; they precede each scene of the libretto, in Volume 1. No attempt was made to present them within accurately drawn frames. Some designs suggest a vertical format, while the surviving photographs indicate that the sets were close to square. Secondly, the set designs were decisively drawn with little evidence of revisions. Occasionally thin, lightly applied lines are visible in these assertive drawings, and in some dark areas of cross-hatching there are indications of other shapes underneath. The motifs are complex enough for some underlying work to be needed to clarify and guide the hand in describing the final form. To draw quite so roughly and firmly Malevich was either preparing a rapid version of what he already knew, perhaps to give to scene painters, or he was deliberately employing a rough execution.

The Set Drawings

The set drawings are surrounded by brief notes, most of which appear to have been written by Malevich but some of these may be later additions. *Victory Over the Sun* has a unique system of numbering its scenes continuously through both parts of the opera, calling them *kartiny* (pictures, also the usual word for Scene). These are grouped into two 'acts', or *deita*, an invented word implying 'actions' or 'doings'.

The six scenes were preceded by an initial curtain that featured images of the protagonist producers of the opera, Matiushin, Kruchenykh, and Malevich, painted onto calico, or a sheet, as described by Benedikt Livshits (in Volume 1).[8] The performance began with the curtain being ripped in two by Futurian Strongmen with triangular heads: 'the curtain rose and the spectator faced a second curtain carrying three hieroglyphs indicating the author, composer, and designer. The music struck up "and these curtains opened for the Prologue".'[9]

Scene 1 in the first Action, or 'Doing', has a backdrop with a fragment of column visible to the left and drapes that hang down. A classical effect is created that may pay homage to Edward Gordon Craig's productions in Russia. The figure of Nero-and-Caligula as one person fits well into this evocation of a classical past. Malevich wrote 'white and black' under this design. This monochrome reference fits the backdrop and the costumes of Nero-Caligula, the Futurian Strongmen, and the Traveller Through All Centuries, although the mood changes when the colourful Bully and Enemies appear.

Next to Scene 1's backdrop Zheverzheev hung the most obviously musical design. It includes two notes on a broken musical stave, together with the curve, perhaps of a string instrument's neck, and a possible bass clef, perhaps with rests above it. Malevich has written alongside the drawing, '2nd scene. Green and black. 1st Doing'. This coincides with the libretto's call for 'green walls and floor'. The drawing is also inscribed 'green up to the funeral'.

The costume designs for Scene 2 are colourful, including the Chorus of singers and Sportsmen. The colour green features in some of the costumes. The Enemy has a green head, for example, and the Certain Person with Bad Intentions has a green top half to his clothes and to his head. The green might have made a pastoral effect evocative of natural landscape, though the effect may have been more shrill and disturbing. In any case, green light projected onto these characters would have made their green areas more or less vanish, leaving what would appear to be only fragmented figures moving around on stage. A Certain Person with Bad Intentions would be halved with only his lower half, rifle and part of his head visible.

Coloured light rays could fragment figures. Malevich had done this in Cubo-Futurist paintings. The Futurist poet, Benedikt Livshits, recalled (in Volume 1) that the play of lights 'gave a certain three-dimensional quality to the costumes that were made from card and wire, transforming the actors into enormous puppets whose movements determined the action'. Indeed, the costumes resemble puppets and their actors move like puppets. As their faces also resemble masks, they have the anonymity of Malevich's peasant images from the lithographs and some of the paintings of 1913, though there is a vivid characterization in the opera costumes. There are, however, no female automata here. These robotic creatures are exclusively male.[10]

Scene 3 is the design with the figures '13'. Here are the Funerarians for the funeral of the sun. Malevich wrote alongside the drawing, 'up to the people conversing'. The figure '13' interested Khlebnikov as the number of lunar months in a year of 366 days, and may pick up the reference to the theatre as Luna[r] Park, implying craziness and lunacy.

The design for Scene 4 was published on the cover of the libretto. It did not appear in Zheverzheev's display and has only recently been discovered in the collection of Nikolai Khardzhiev, now in the Stedelijk Museum, Amsterdam. The design features the great sun/eye motif cut in half as its final eclipse commences. The eye motif was frequently associated with the sun in Russian Futurist works, for example, in Kamensky's *Ferro-concrete* poem,

The Sun Lubok (right), where the sun is inscribed 'sun brightness = the face of genius', while the Futurists are associated with the moon. The split-eye motif, on the other hand, seems in part to be a play on the archaic Russian word for eye, *oko,* and the word for window, *okno*. In Malevich's portraits of the painter Ivan Kliun in 1913, one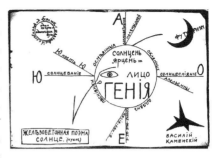
eye reveals a rural scene, a wooden hut and a window. The split-eye motif had also featured on Malevich's cover for *The Three* (in Volume 1).

A photograph of Scene 4 on stage reproduced in *Early Morning* confirms the sequence of designs, as the photograph includes the funeral attendants with the big eye of the sun behind them (in Volume 1). Around this sun images of flight and the cosmos appear. On the libretto cover this design carries also the Cyrillic letters '*Kp*' (Kr). The sun captured, Doing One ends with a curtain, about which we know nothing. It was perhaps the theatre's own front curtain.

By the end of Doing One (1st *Deito*) the Futurists have captured, killed, and buried the sun, the source and sustainer of life on earth. What follows in Doing Two (2nd *Deito*) is grim and bleak.

The curtain opens to reveal the sunless world perceived by the Futurians and enforced by their Strongmen. The backdrop for Scene 5 is unlike the others. It features a rectangle that initially appears divided diagonally into a black triangle and a white triangle. A student of Malevich reported that this is not so: 'the line dividing black from white is slightly bent downwards to cross the lower edge of the rectangle … [so that the white area] is seen as part of the great sun'.[11] This effect would be strengthened by the proper use of lighting.

The Sun Carriers heave their load without showing it. Malevich has altered the numbering on this design and he or another hand has added the word *kvadrat* (square, quadrilateral). The set design has no colour, but the costumes give clues. The New Man and his colleagues wear the colours formerly worn by the Enemies, purple, black and yellow, with a green face. The Cowards hide their faces and wear yellow, and the Fat Man strides anxiously about in red, white and purple, his face half-purple, half-green. In the midst of this is the Reader. These are colourful people in the new sunless world, some of them desperate and others confident. Their varied colours would move from the black to the white backgrounds, fragmented by lights.

The design for the last scene resembles a kind of Cubist house.

Oddly, this corresponds substantially to an oil painting by Malevich, *Musical Instrument/ Lamp* (Stedelijk Museum Amsterdam), and is perhaps an allusion to the opera itself. The Fat Man reappears and the Old Resident puzzles at the new perspectives after the sun's departure. Young figures appear to replace them. Here come the Sportsmen, the Aviator once more, and the Futurian Strongmen who were present at the start. This is their new world. Their house is seen in the backdrop, viewed largely from above, as the Aviator might just have seen it, racing past its roof, chimneys, window, and clock in his  precipitate descent. Malevich may have depicted the Aviator's flight in his lithograph *Universal Landscape* (above) of 1913, published in Kruchenykh's book, *The Poetry of V. Mayakovsky*, where window lights and reflections in all directions are drawn in different perspectives. The house in the opera was inside out, and its windows looked inwards onto the Universe.[12] All of the designs for the 1913 production of *Victory Over the Sun* break new territory in stage design. Nothing like them had been seen before. They substantially predated the wartime experiments of Giacomo Balla in Stravinsky's *Fireworks* performed in 1917, Pablo Picasso's innovative designs for Erik Satie and Jean Cocteau's ballet *Parade* in 1917, or Léger's 1922 designs for Darius Milhaud's *Creation of the World*. Malevich's use of coloured spotlights and stiff, fragmented figures to go with Futurist music and *zaum* words represent an unprecedented collaboration, radical in each and all of its disciplines.

Interpreting the Scenes

Given the radical nature of the opera, is it possible to identify a coherent narrative and formal structure that underpins the two acts, the Doings? The presence of the Traveller Through All Centuries in the first and last Scenes binds events of the ancient past and present, and suggests that the understanding of these temporal links are derived from his knowledge of all dimensions. This philosophical reference was a familiar theme in Russian Futurism, but anathema in Italian Futurism.

All of the designs incorporate a frame-like structure surrounding the roughly rectangular area of the central shapes and images. This can be seen as a perspective box. The diagonals that join the outer corners to those of the central rectangle can be seen as the receding perspective lines of a box. Even on a flat surface, as shown in the two newspaper photographs from *Early Morning* in Volume 1, they encourage what the Futurist Benedikt Livshits called 'pictorial stereometry' (also in Volume 1). This framework persists from the Old World of Scene 1, through to the multi-dimensional world of the last Scene.

In the design that Malevich made for Scene 1, the mixture of Nero and Caligula speaks before a backdrop that not only incorporated fragmented suggestions of the classical past, but also included geometric forms that seemed to hang in the air as they cross the perspective lines of the illusionistic box. Reports of the need for a piano at the last moment for the production suggest hasty readjustments to the production or to the finances of *Victory*, so perhaps Malevich implied the wings, flies, and floor of the stage with his perspective 'box', although they were actually painted flat on the backdrop, as the newspaper photographs indicate. With the aid of lighting, they may, therefore, have been strong enough to sustain the pictorial illusion of receding space on the stage. The rectangles crossing the lines of the perspective box could appear to float in the air in a wholly unclassical way, making the link with later generations, and incidentally heightening the banter on stage about the fossilized conventions of academic art stifling new creation.

In the scenes of Doing One this perspective box surrounds a flat central area, depicting a platform, musical motifs, the declining sun, and the half-eclipsed and beautiful great eye of the captured sun. In these scenes the action and setting are characterized with fragmentary references to Classicism, the end of perspective, and victory over the sun. The frames carry supporting ideas, including the column in Scene 1, the rhythmic repetitions in Scene 2, descending darkness in Scene 3, and elements of the Aviator's flight and planetary space in Scene 4.

The new era presented in Doing Two, however, is different. The centre of Scene 5 has an empty frame around it. The new world of the Futurians in Scene 6 shows a multi-dimensional house bursting from the flat central rectangle, pushing in front of the frame and towards the audience in the theatre, projecting and not receding. This house burgeons confidently forward, the busiest and most dynamic of the sets for the opera. Under his drawing Malevich has simply written 'house'. The drawings exemplify the dismantling of Classical academic rules, including the convention that linear and atmospheric perspective credibly describe a single time and place. The sun no longer throws its shadows in consistent directions, and the vanishing point is no longer to be found on the horizon. Now it opens out in all directions and times. Killing the sun wrecks gravity and diurnal notions of time. Time and space become relative to other times and places, impermanent and shifting, a feature of the viewers' gaze and no longer the familiar and credible illusion supplied by the tricks of old fixed viewpoints. Doing One concludes with the transformation of time and space. The old Western conventions lose their authority.

Doing Two opens onto the darkness of infinite and measureless space. Scale, direction, and time have become relative. The newspaper photograph of Scene 4 (*Early Morning*, in Volume 1) shows calculations inscribed lower left, equivalent to those made by Khlebnikov to determine the cyclic rhythms of battles in history and the speed of heartbeats on other planets. After the demise of the sun, time and space need new measures.

There is no sign here of the Italian Futurists' contemporary enthusiasm for speed. This is, by contrast, cosmological. *Victory Over the Sun* envisaged humanity making its own way through time and space. The old order is relinquished (and this may have implied also the Tsar), revealed as an illusion from a simpler world-view: 'I want to say everything – recollect the past full of the sorrows of mistakes… the breaking and bending of knees… let us remember it and compare it with the present… so joyous: liberated from the heaviness of universal gravity we can imaginatively arrange our belongings as if a rich kingdom were being moved.'[13] (Scene 5.)

The new order is immensely diverse, complicated, and dynamic. The sun that divided yesterday from today and tomorrow was captured and killed. The funeral attendants wear a black square on their chest, and the Futurist Aviator flies on through the vast continuity of time and space.

Alternative Perspectives

There is another way of looking at these designs for *Victory Over the Sun*. On the printed libretto, Malevich's design for Scene 4 appeared with the great sun/ eye and the Cyrillic letters 'Kr' for the librettist's name Kruchenykh. There are other references to the opera's creative team. Scene 1 may be exceptional as it represents the Old World. Matiushin is represented by music in Scene 2. Malevich was working on a painting of Matiushin at this time. Scene 3 with its figure '13' may represent Khlebnikov. Scene 4 acknowledges Kruchenykh as author of the libretto. Scene 5, part of the New Order, shows Malevich working with new, radical and simple means. Finally Scene 6 features the world of the Aviator's space-time. This was Kamensky's role, and although he did write *zaum* verse, it was Kruchenykh who wrote the Aviator's *zaum* utterances here. In this view, *Victory Over the Sun* celebrates the Futurists themselves. This fits well with descriptions of portraits painted on the curtain torn down to begin the show. Khlebnikov, Matiushin, Kruchenykh, Malevich and Kamensky are all represented. Malevich's oil painting *Aviator* (State Russian Museum, St. Petersburg) reflects this identification of Kamensky.

There are other Futurist figures to consider. The red letterpress poster (in Volume 1) for the Futurist theatre productions was constructed around a lithograph in black by David Burliuk. He used it another way up in the miscellany, *Trap for Judges II* (*Sadok Sudei II*), and on the back cover of the published libretto. David Burliuk showed movement by repeating the lines of the tree, horse, and man. This already announced an energetic world with no fixed concept of the right way up.

When the creators of *Victory Over the Sun* had their photographs taken, they inverted furniture (in Volume 1). In some of these group photographs David Burliuk also appears in the absurd formality of Futurist dress (right), the conventional top hat and waistcoat of the urban sophisticate, with a red spoon in the breast pocket, a radish in the lapel, or a cat painted across his face.

This Futurist top hat appears three times in connection with the opera. It appears in red on the head of attendants at the funeral of the sun, who also have a black square as the top of their costumes. One eye is blocked out, and Burliuk had only one eye. Burliuk, though neither writer nor performer of *Victory Over the Sun,* was a presence behind the enterprise, a fact acknowledged visually in the red poster and on the back cover of the libretto. He reappears on the lithographic poster in colour made by Olga Rozanova (in Volume 1). As Kruchenykh's partner she knew well the *Victory Over the Sun* project and all his aims for it. Her poster announced 'the world's first productions of Futurist theatre', in rugged lettering reminiscent of that used by Malevich on the cover of *The Three*. Her scattered green lettering spells out *Futur Teatr* (or 'Future Theatre'). In the great arc above is the curve of the Futurist's belly. It is written, so to speak, on his waistcoat. The surrounding black is his formal black jacket, and (upper left) is the black top hat. His hands reach round upper right and centre by the lower edge. This is a homage to David Burliuk, alive with energy, as the so-called father of Russian Futurism.

Much the same figure appears in the *Englishman in Moscow* (Stedelijk Museum Amsterdam, right), a painting by Malevich closely related to *Victory* in its imagery, words and ideas. Malevich hides one eye and presents the black top hat square in elevation. There is the waistcoat and a spoon, visible in a documentary photograph, and once apparently attached to the painting. The figure is partially eclipsed by other images and the canvas bears the words 'Partial Eclipse' in Russian. The sun had actually been eclipsed in recent memory. Here the words evoke fragmentation and refer to time, as the word partial (*chastichnoe*) includes the fragment (*chas* / hour, watch, clock).

In the painting, this top-hatted figure perhaps walks along Kuznetsky Most (Kuznetsky Bridge) provoking the crowds as Burliuk did in real life. Street signs may indicate the images that lie before and behind him. The racing club lies behind him as he approaches the fishmonger, church and barracks. Or perhaps they simply figure in his mind. In either case, military imagery dominates the foreground. Much of this fits *Victory Over the Sun* and fed into it or came out of it, we do not yet know which. *Englishman in Moscow* is Malevich's homage to David Burliuk. It was not exhibited until it appeared in Tramway V: The First Futurist Exhibition of Paintings, which opened in St. Petersburg on 3 March 1915.

Malevich made many references to his Futurist friends in the drawings and paintings related to his designs for the opera. The newspaper photograph of Scene 1 (*Early Morning*, in Volume 1) shows part of the letter P (equivalent to the Latin letter R). A related drawing and a painting incorporate the Cyrillic letters OBP (that is OVR), the initials of Olga Vladimirovna Rozanova. Why Malevich associated Rozanova with Scene 1 remains a mystery. He may also have made reference to Tatlin, Kliun, and even Picasso. It is not easy to untangle these hidden messages and their ambiguities, but they cannot be dismissed as accidental. The designs identify individual Futurists with particular scenes and aspects of the opera.

The pre-set curtain, with its portraits of Khlebnikov, Kruchenykh, Matiushin and Malevich, presented the opera's creators to the audience, a rare and extraordinary gesture, destroyed almost at once when the Futurian Strongmen violently ripped it down. By then the opera was launched and its creators were part of the spectacle. They continued to haunt the action and the design as creators, in some cases as performers, and as subjects of the spectacle. Their collaboration was part of the narrative of the opera as well as its means of creation.

The vital involvement of the painter Malevich in *Victory Over the Sun* had an immense impact in Russian theatre. Sergei Diaghilev made artists essential contributors to his ballet productions, and the Kamerny (Chamber) Theatre, that opened its doors in Moscow in 1914 under the director Alexander Tairov, immediately adopted Alexandra Exter and Alexander Vesnin. These painters, who knew Malevich and his work well, became a crucial part of Tairov's creative team. *Victory Over the Sun* was a fundamental step in artists' inventive and equal input into Russian theatre. Beyond that it established the stage as an arena for the creativity of the visual artist in a way that has influenced painters of the stage ever since.

Notes

1   The publications had a print run of 350 and 1,000 respectively.

2   At this *Union of Youth* exhibition, Malevich exhibited his paintings of village workers, depicted with cone-shaped forms, including the *Woman with Buckets* and *Morning in the Village after the Storm*. He also exhibited paintings of woodcutters with their saws, and the *Completed Portrait of Ivan Kliunkov*. Kliunkov, or Ivan Kliun, worked closely with Malevich. This series Malevich called *zaum realism*, which culminated with the *Knifegrinder*. They were on view during the period of the opera, but none of them displays related imagery. *Cubo-Futurism* was adopted in Russia for work that responded to both Parisian Cubist and Italian Futurist techniques and was first used in October 1912. Dmitrii Sarabianov distinguishes a dynamic stage and then a more static, constructed stage in the Cubo-Futurism of Malevich in 1913, in which the 'principle of sequential movement' was not necessarily evident. Malevich used the term *Cubo-Futurist Realism* in the catalogue of the Union of Youth exhibition in November 1913. See D. Sarabjanov 'Malevic tra cubismo francese e futurismo italiano' in *Polifonia: da Malevic a Tat'jana Bruni 1910-1930. Bozzetti teatrali dell'avanguardi russa* (Milan: Electa, 1998), exhibition catalogue.

3   The large comma visible in the photograph on the cover was reversed in the published version.

4   Susan P. Compton, *The World Backwards. Russian Futurist Books*

1912-1916 (London: The British Library, 1978), 53. See Volume 1 of this collection.

5   Duchamp was later involved in the purchase of Malevich's painting *Knifegrinder* for the collection of the Société Anonyme, now at Yale University Art Gallery.

6   This is discussed thoroughly in Nicoletta Misler, 'Il Colore del spazio' in *Polifonia: da Malevic a Tat'jana Bruni 1910-1930* [2], 38-44.

7   The Zheverzheev Collection, including the designs for *Victory Over the Sun*, are now housed in the State Museum of Theatre Arts, St. Petersburg.

8   Benedikt Livshits in *The One and a Half Eyed Archer*, cited and discussed in Alma H. Law, 'Vittoria sul sole: note sugli allestimenti del 1913 e 1920' in *Polifonia: da Malevic a Tat'jana Bruni 1910-1930* [2], 34. The libretto mentions curtains at the start, after the first half, and at the end.

9   Described by A. Magebrov and cited by John Milner in *Malevich and the Art of Geometry* (New Haven and London: Yale University Press, 1996), 91. See also Dzhon E. Boult [John E. Bowlt], *Khudozhniki Russkogo Teatra 1880-1930. Katalog-Rezone. Stat'i. Knyaz' N. D. Lobanov-Rostovsky ob istorii kollektsii* (Moscow: Isskustvo, 1994), 196.

10   The art historian Valentine Marcadé described the opera as 'dynamic sculpture'. See Valentine Marcadé, *Le Renouveu de l'art pictural russe 1863-1914* (Lausanne: L'Age d'Homme, 1971), 254. John E. Bowlt also stressed 'the three-dimensional kinetic whole' that was *Victory Over the Sun*. See Boult [Bowlt], *Khudozhniki Russkogo Teatra* [9], 43.

11   Cited by Boult [Bowlt], *Khudozhniki russkogo Teatra* [9], 194.

12   Benois' designs for Diaghilev's production of Igor Stravinsky's *Petrushka* in Paris in 1911 should not be ignored here. They have the fairground quality, the puppet-like performers, an inside-out room featuring starlit walls, and devils on the doors as frightening as any of Goncharova's, Malevich's, or Rozanova's illustrations to the publication *A Game in Hell*.

13   The phrase, *the world upside down,* was used from the eighteenth century and earlier to denote an absurd world in which unexpected things occur through role-reversal, where a goose may cook a man, for example. Chap books in Britain and *lubok* prints in Russia embraced this absurd imagery for entertainment, children's books, song sheets and satirical prints, such as the famous *lubok* of the *Mice Burying the Cat* that satirized Peter the Great. This popular imagery was attractive to Larionov, Goncharova, Malevich, and Rozanova. The Futurist book, *Worldbackwards*, may imply the same concept, and *Victory Over the Sun* as a whole has an absurd aspect like the World Upside Down. It is after all a strange story where men kill the sun to live in bleak darkness of their own making. Political or social satire is not out of the question here. It might explain David Burliuk's absurd version of well-to-do urban clothes. John E. Bowlt related the opera to the tradition of theatrical fairground booths, a Cubo-Futurist *Balagan* (show booth) at the *Yarmaka* (fair). Boult [Bowlt], *Khudozhniki Russkogo Teatra* [9], 44.

THE MUSIC

'In music: new ideas of harmony and of melody, new pitch (quarter of a tone), simultaneous movement of four completely independent voices (Reger, Schoenberg).'

Mikhail Matiushin, 'Futurism in St. Petersburg: Performances on the 2nd, 3rd, 4th, and 5th of December 1913', *First Journal of Russian Futurists*, January 1914

Christopher Dempsey

A MUSICAL ASSESSMENT OF
VICTORY OVER THE SUN

In December 1913, the Luna Park Theatre in St. Petersburg played host to four nights of Futurist performances.

On the first and third nights a new play called *Vladimir Mayakovsky: A Tragedy* was premiered with the writer, Mayakovsky himself, in the principal role.

On the other nights a new work, the opera *Victory Over the Sun* (*Pobeda nad Solntsem*), was premiered. Those responsible for this work, a libretto by Aleksei Kruchenykh with a Prologue by Velimir Khlebnikov, sets and costumes by the artist Kazimir Malevich, and music by Mikhail Matiushin, had already begun making names for themselves in the avant-garde movements in Russia.

In later years, art historians would trace the beginnings of Suprematism, an art movement that began in 1915, to the sets by Malevich, while literary scholars would look at the libretto as an example of Futurist drama. Music historians, however, did not have the same opportunity to provide interpretations because most of the music eventually disappeared only to have parts of it rediscovered by art historians in the early 1980s. Consequently, there has not been any examination into whether the music of *Victory Over the Sun* contributed to the fabric of Russian avant-garde music of the early 20th century, or indeed whether the music should merit the same academic attention as the other aspects of the opera. This article provides the first steps toward such an examination.

It is difficult to make conclusive observations about the 1913 production of *Victory Over the Sun*. First, it was a truly avant-garde piece drawing on multiple fields, and because of its modernist tendencies, there is a gap between theory and application that applies to costume sketches vs. actual attire, desired performing forces vs. actual forces, desired results in the libretto and score vs. the final results, and a host of others. The objective of the work also creates problems because the Futurist Theatre placed as much emphasis on audience participation and reactions as it did to the production itself. Above all else, it is difficult to determine what music was actually performed during the performance, whether there were slight alterations to the libretto, or even on the nights the events occurred. To illustrate this difficulty, consider the problems of the existing source material of the music.

Source Material

The original music that was used during the 1913 performance is still unaccounted for. The libretto, published in 1913 shortly after the performance, has long provided the framework of the opera. Besides reproducing the opera's text, it contains several valuable clues including stage directions and a differentiation between spoken and sung lines. It also offers some examples of the music including a two-measure introduction, two songs, another musical fragment called 'Notes of the Futurians' that uses quarter-tones, and a brief explanation of Matiushin's quarter-tone notation (all in Volume 1).[1] Other than identifying the sections that are sung, the libretto gives no further insight as to the remaining music of the opera.

A second source of music consists of fifteen pages of manuscript discovered by Christiane Bauermeister in 1981 while she was in the Soviet Union and they were printed without commentary in a book in 1983, and have been reproduced in this collection in Volume 1.[2] A subsequent examination revealed that these pages are not autograph manuscripts, however, but rather copies in the hand of Maria Ender, a painter and student of Matiushin.[3] Since Ender and Matiushin did not meet until 1916, three years after the opera's performance, this manuscript must be a copy of another, possibly lost, source.[4] Both songs present in the libretto appear in the manuscript, but with very slight alterations that suggest copying errors or minor revisions.[5] Since none of these differences drastically alters the structure of the songs, it is reasonable to assume that the manuscripts represent an accurate version of the opera.

It is not clear when Ender copied this music or why. It has already been established that it must have been copied after 1916, but it could have been written as late as 1942, the year she died.[6] It is possible she made this copy between 1922 and 1923 – years that correspond to another planned performance of the opera. In 1923, the artist El Lissitzky wanted to create what he called an 'electro-mechanical' version of *Victory Over the Sun* in Germany. He made several sketches for the characters, but production never proceeded beyond these initial stages. Lissitzky refers to both the libretto and the music in an essay written about this project during the same year:

> For the first presentation of this electromechanical peepshow I have used a modern play, which was still, however, written for the stage. It is the futurist opera 'Victory Over the Sun' by A. Kruchenykh who originated sound-poetry and is the leading writer of the most modern Russian poetic work. The opera was presented for the first time in 1913, in Petersburg. The music is by Matiushin (quarter-tones). Malevich painted the scenery (the curtain = black square).[7]

Lissitzky could have requested copies of the original music from Matiushin for this performance, and Ender, who was still one of Matiushin's students at that time, would have been a logical choice for scribe. Direct contact between Lissitzky and Matiushin has not been documented, but Lissitzky was in contact with Mayakovsky, having designed the cover and page-spreads for his *For the Voice* (*Dlya Golosa)*. Mayakovsky also maintained contact with Khlebnikov and Kruchenykh through this period and any one of them could have acted as an intermediary between Lissitzky and Matiushin. It is possible that Lissitzky either cancelled his request for copies after they were made but before they were sent, thus keeping them in Russia, or an additional copy was made that remained behind.

Another possibility is a studio performance by students of UNOVIS in the Vitebsk Practical Art Institute and directed by Malevich in 1920, while still another possibility concerns the private performances Matiushin organized between 1920 and 1923 at the apartment of the Enders to honour the memory of Matiushin's wife, Elena Guro. These performances used Matiushin's earlier compositions in the production, and it is possible that this music was used for one of them.[8]

Looking towards the non-musical source material, there appear several commentaries, published from within days after the premiere to decades after, which discuss the opera, its preparation and its performance. Numerous newspaper articles, published as early as a few days prior to the performance to shortly afterward, provide views of those unrelated to the performance.[9] These are important because they are among the only sources that are relatively untainted by Futurist bias. Matiushin's recollections appeared about a month after the performance (in Volume 1).[10] In them, he discussed the novelties of the music, preparation of the spectacle, the performance and its aftermath. Kruchenykh's commentaries appeared in his memoirs in which he discussed the libretto and its treatment of text, and methods for its performance (in Volume 1).[11] The memoirs of Benedikt

Livshits show a viewpoint from a Futurist not involved in the performance (in Volume 1).[12] And finally, the recollections of K. Tomashevsky, which appeared over twenty years after the performance, reveal some thoughts of one of the actors.[13]

Background

Mikhail Vasilievich Matiushin was born in Nizhnii Novgorod in 1861. Although he is best known for his paintings, publications, and artistic theories on his approach to a heightened awareness of the natural world through scientific reasoning, which he called 'Spatial Realism', his early life prepared him for a career in music. He attended the Moscow Conservatory from 1876 to 1881. Upon leaving the Conservatory, he became a violinist with the Court Orchestra of St. Petersburg, a post he maintained until 1913. Around 1898, Matiushin began to pursue his interest in art by joining the Society for the Encouragement of the Arts where he first met Elena Guro, whom he would later marry, and the painter-theorist Vladimir Markov. He left the society in 1905 and began attending the Zvantseva School for Art, where he studied under Léon Bakst and Mstislav Dobuzhinsky. Matiushin began his association with experimental art in 1909 when he joined Nikolai Kulbin's Impressionist group in St. Petersburg.

In that year, Matiushin also met some of the figures who would soon become the Futurists, including the Burliuk brothers (David, Nikolai, and Vladimir) and through them, Vasili Kamensky and Khlebnikov. Matiushin helped organise the Union of Youth, a Futurist society based in St. Petersburg, but he also maintained contact with the Impressionists until 1910. Shortly after this break, Matiushin met the other Futurists, Kruchenykh and Malevich. The collaboration of these men led to the opera *Victory Over the Sun*, which was developed during the summer of 1913 in Uusikirkko, Finland.

The performances of *Victory Over the Sun* and Mayakovsky's play took place over a four-night period between December 2 and 5, 1913 at the Luna Park Theatre in St. Petersburg. Each work appeared on alternating nights beginning with Mayakovsky's play. The cast was mostly amateurs – students who had responded to an advertisement for participants. The performances were sold out and, unlike other nights with entertainment sponsored by the Futurists, there was no rioting.[14] The press, however, attacked the works, the gathering, and the actors' performance. Some referred to the 'lack of talent' and the 'endless nonsense' of the performance, while others used the occasion as an opportunity to dismiss the Futurists themselves.[15]

Although the collaborators called *Victory Over the Sun* an opera, it actually has very few ties to Western operatic tradition. Instead, it represents the next step beyond what had previously been attempted in Futurist theatre. 'Futurist Evenings', the previous manifestation of Futurist Entertainment, presented a way of experimenting with theatrical ideas while providing a forum for their works and manifestos.[16] First organised in 1913, they realised many of the ideas set forth in the first manifesto on theatre by Marinetti called 'The Variety Theatre'. Marinetti discarded earlier notions of theatre in favour of ones that embrace the merging of different genres – the circus, cabaret, and music hall – into a new theatrical experience. This 'total theatre' requires the use of lighting, colour, sound, noise, speech, and movement that create dynamic tension and would allow the audience to perceive the entire performance simultaneously. Alogical sequences of events, characters, text, and décor were of primary importance to the Futurists since these elements destroyed suspension of disbelief and thus made the performance more realistic by concentrating on the performance as an entity itself.[17]

In addition to Futurist theatre, which is discussed in greater detail elsewhere in this collection, a major influence on *Victory Over the Sun* was the Russian cabaret that had been gaining popularity among almost all classes of the Russian people since the founding of the first cabaret in 1908.[18] That cabaret, The Bat founded by Nikita Baliev in Moscow, paved the way for others including two St. Petersburg cabarets: The Crooked Mirror and The Stray Dog. The Crooked Mirror also formed in 1908 by Alexander Kugel' and his wife Zinaida Kholmskaia, while The Stray Dog formed at the end of 1911 by Nikolai Evreinov, Boris Pronin, and Nikolai Kulbin, whose Impressionist group Matiushin had belonged to from 1909 to 1910. The entertainment at these cabarets was not unlike that of their Western European counterparts with 'a confined stage housed in a small restaurant or café providing a variety of sequences sometimes with topical social and political significance.'[19] But in the Russian version, improvisatory performance, audience participation, and a quick succession of acts took on a greater importance. Additionally, the incorporation of clowning, acrobatics, and pantomime turned the cabaret into a continuation of Russian folk-theatre.[20] Consequently, the folk influences of the theatre affected the music performed there as shorter songs and melodies dominated. The music changed as the acts did, while occasional interludes were improvised in between these songs.

This sequence of songs and interludes provided a template for *Victory Over the Sun*, which closely follows this pattern. Ultimately, *Victory Over the Sun* should not be considered an opera in the traditional sense, but rather a piece of Futurist theatre that borrows musical styles from popular entertainment of the time.

The influence of the cabaret shows that the theoretical constructs behind the Futurist ideas of theatre eventually gave way to more realistic considerations when put into practice. Like *zaum*, it also presented an avenue for the Russians to step out from the shadows of the Italians and do something that, although borrowing from the Italians, remained unique to the Russians. The Russian Futurists had attended The Stray Dog in the months leading up to the performance of *Victory* and the style of music was familiar to them. Although the incorporation of music from a folk-dominated cabaret may seem contradictory to avant-garde ideas, it is important to keep in mind that several members of avant-garde art movements frequented cabarets, and the works performed at these establishments may have obtained a sense of modernism by virtue of their clientele. In this respect, the Futurists saw the advantages of borrowing musical styles of the cabaret as something that both retained avant-garde characteristics and remained independent of the Italians, while also fitting within the framework of a workable template.

Musical Considerations

The existing music to the opera (in Volume 1) is written for voices with a piano accompaniment only. There are several songs that are separated by musical interludes. The songs are distinct from one another and are usually no more than ten measures in length. This music, coupled with stage directions provided in the libretto, has made it possible to estimate that over half the music for the opera may be missing.

To illustrate how the missing sections were determined, consider the first music that appears in the manuscript fragments. Its text corresponds to a section labeled 'singing' on page six of the libretto; however, the libretto indicates three other 'singing' sections prior to this one: the first on page four, the second on page five, and the third on page six just above the existing song. Complicating this matter, however, is Matiushin's use of three methods to express the text: singing, speech, and speech over musical accompaniment (melodrama). Fortunately, a key piece of information that helped estimate how much of the opera is missing can be found on the fourteenth and fifteenth pages of the fragments where the numbers '11' and '12' appear on the upper right hand and upper left hand corners respectively. They are probably page numbers, and though it is impossible to make conclusive observations without the actual manuscript, their locations imply that these two pages are found on the front and back of the same sheet of paper. These numbers are too low to be pages for the entire opera, but they may represent pages for the second act. Why they only appear on these two pages, and who put them there and why, have yet to be determined. If they do represent page numbers, and if we assume that all the other sheets are the same way, i.e., front and back of a single sheet, then it is possible to estimate that between 9 to 16 pages of the opera are missing.[21]

Surviving sources are not always consistent with the numerous commentaries that the collaborators and participants published following the opera's performance. One of these involves the question of instrumentation. Both the existing sources are scored for only piano, but about a month after the opera's performance, Matiushin published an article (in Volume 1) in which he discussed the opera first as an example of the new changes in art, music and literature, but then addressed the difficulties that he and his collaborators faced while trying to organise the performances. One passage suggests that Matiushin orchestrated the opera:

> For the opera and the tragedy they recruited students who were amateur performers. Experienced singers sang only two leading parts in the opera. There was a very bad chorus of seven people, only three of whom could sing—the management, ignoring our insistence and requests, hired them only two days before the performance. Considering the intricacy of the composition, it was impossible to prepare anything well. A broken, out of tune piano, substituting for an orchestra, was delivered on the day of the performance.[22]

Matiushin's reference to the piano as a substitution for an orchestra may imply that an orchestra was originally intended for the performance, but all that could be obtained was a piano; however, the 'management' that Matiushin refers to is the Union of Youth, the organisers of the performance. The article criticises them by decrying the number of rehearsals and pointing out that Malevich did not have the materials he wanted. The tone of the article vividly portrays the growing differences between the ideas of the Union of Youth and those of Matiushin and the others. The differences climaxed early in 1914, a few months after the performances, when the two groups terminated their short-lived alliance. Matiushin could be indicating their original desire to have an orchestra, while using the piano as a way to lay blame on the Union of Youth.

Despite Matiushin's insinuation that the music required an orchestra, additional evidence strongly suggests that he did not orchestrate the opera. The music often features idioms common to the piano, including parallel octaves, glissandos, and rhythmic patterns. Furthermore, the music encompasses a tremendous range, with frequent occurrences of extremely low notes following extremely high ones. Other known works by Matiushin support the idea that the opera was not orchestrated since they show that he preferred writing for the piano, violin and voice. The music to *Harlekin*, a play by Elena Guro from her book *Barrel Organ* (*Sharmanka*) and published in 1909, is for piano solo, *Don Quixot'* is a five movement suite for piano with an added voice in one movement and a violin in another, while *Autumn Dream* (*Osenii Son*) is a suite for violin and piano. Both these pieces were published in 1915. One other work, an opera by the same collaborators called *Victorious War* (*Pobezhdennaia voina*), was abandoned and it is not known whether Matiushin ever composed any music for it.[23]

Without question, the best known musical aspect of *Victory Over the Sun* is its use of quarter-tones, but a critical examination of source material casts doubt on whether their use was intentional, or simply a consequence of the available performing forces that the Futurists promoted to their advantage following the premiere, when references to quarter-tones actually began to surface. In 1914, Matiushin referred to quarter-tones in his article when he described the music as 'new ideas of harmony and melody, new pitch (quarter of a tone), simultaneous movement of four completely independent voices (Reger, Schoenberg).'[24] At the end of 1913 the libretto was published, which included the 'Notes of the Futurians' fragment with quarter-tones and an explanation of the notation, and both were reproduced in the collection *The Three* (*Troe*, published September 1913*)*.

'Notes of the Futurians' Fragment. Explanation of notation on top.

Yet with the exception of this fragment, there are no other quarter-tones in the surviving music and it is not clear how the fragment was used, if at all. The word 'Futurians' first appears in the Prologue and again in the first scene to describe the Strongmen, who are subsequently referred to by that name, but there is nowhere that the fragment's description, or the phrase below the music, 'transition of blue and black,' corresponds to the libretto.

The remaining sources show neither the special notation for quarter-tones, nor sections of super-chromaticism, with a note between two notes a semitone apart as in the Futurian fragment, where quarter-tones could be inferred.

Furthermore, the opera's performing forces cast additional doubts on the use of quarter-tones. First, it doesn't seem unreasonable to question the singing abilities of the mostly amateur cast that the Futurists obtained for their performance. Indeed, whether their cast could actually sing in tune diatonically, even without microtones, seems to be an assumption too often accepted. Second, the piano, as apparently intended instrumentation and as actual performing force, makes a rather poor choice for a piece with quarter-tones, especially when the piano arrives on the day of the performance broken and out of tune. Unlike other instruments, where a player has an opportunity to slightly raise or lower a pitch through finger placement or embouchure adjustments to produce a microtonal pitch, the piano does not allow the performer to adjust pitches while playing. Microtones *are* possible on a piano, but only as a result of tuning specific notes slightly sharp or flat prior to performance. Since a piano is limited to playing only as many pitches as it has keys, a chromatic pitch would have to disappear for every microtonal pitch added. Consequently, the super-chromatic run in the 'Notes of the Futurians' fragment, while theoretically possible, would create an instrument with a tuning system that would not work for the rest of the opera.

Perhaps the Futurists, in realising during rehearsals the difficulties of producing the opera as it was originally intended, opted to take advantage of these shortcomings by promoting them as new ideas in music. Here, out of tune singers and pianos became practitioners of quarter-tones, while rhythmic irregularities became independent voices. The recollections of Tomashevsky, which suggest that the singers had to contend with these intervals, also help to support this idea:

> The most important role of the Aviator was sung by the then well-known tenor, Richter, who was an artist from the People's House...
> At first Richter felt uncomfortable when he had to intentionally sing

off pitch. But later he became used to it and honestly performed that Futurist nuance.[25]

Tomashevsky portrays Richter as one of the only trained singers to participate in this production, and it is reasonable to assume that he could have sung in tune given his implied success at the People's House, yet Tomashevsky's recollection is that Richter was intentionally instructed to sing off pitch. While this could indicate that the Aviator's songs used Matiushin's notation for quarter-tones, the surviving music shows that this is not the case. More likely, it suggests that he was asked to alter the chromatic notes already on the page by a quarter-tone, thereby intentionally singing off pitch. If this is correct, then it would indicate that the introduction of quarter-tones occurred during the production stage and not the compositional stage – a response to the quality of performers. In this interpretation, Matiushin's quarter-tones and other 'new ideas' in music were not premeditated, but rather were developed organically by accident during the production of *Victory Over the Sun* and therefore could be promoted by the Futurists only after the premiere.

Matiushin's autobiography, written shortly before his death in 1934, also argues against quarter-tones. In it he states that although the idea of quarter-tones came to him in the years 1904/1905, he did not implement it until 1915 in a method book entitled *Guide to Studying Quarter-tones for Violin*, which uses similar quarter-tone notation as the 'Futurians' fragment.[26]

Example from *Guide to Studying Quarter-tones for Violin* with similar notation.

That Matiushin does not mention the opera at all in discussing his use of quarter-tones is telling. The suggestion that Matiushin's time lag between idea and implementation may be somewhat inflated in an attempt to backdate the creation of quarter-tones is supported by two events that in the years preceding seem to be immediate precursors to the idea of quarter-tones in an opera. In 1910, Arthur Lourié composed a string quartet with quarter-tones in St. Petersburg,[27] while in 1912, the Italian Futurist, Francesco Balilla Pratella, published the 'Technical Manifesto of Futurist Music' where he suggested the use of rhythmic irregularity, atonality, and microtones.[28]

While it is possible that Matiushin was unaware of Lourié's composition – Lourié completed his studies at St. Petersburg Conservatory in 1913 and was introduced to Livshits and the Futurists in the weeks following the performance[29] – it is very likely that he knew about the manifesto since the Russian Futurists examined much of what came out of Italy. Indeed, there is little difficulty in finding examples in Matiushin's opera of the Italian manifesto's other recommendations. Rhythmic irregularity occurs in syncopated sections, but mostly in the text placement, where words may begin on offbeats of not only eighth notes, but multiple tuplets as well. Consequently, textual and musical accents fall at different times, creating a constant tug-of-war between the two forces. Most songs are written for a soloist or a homorhythmic choir: no duets or other songs requiring interplay between voices occur throughout the opera. The interludes rely heavily on ostinati and are often just a one- or two-measure pattern repeated or sequenced in some manner until the next section. During these interludes, the characters continue with their lines, but in a melodramatic fashion – spoken over the music – instead of recitative. Dissonance dominates the music as chords often include additional notes unrelated to the triads. Matiushin often favours dyads of major and minor seconds in order to increase the dissonant qualities of his lines, especially in thinner textures. The opera lacks any overall tonal plan, but some sections, particularly the songs, have some sense of tonality. It is possible that the tonal relationship here is meant to mimic the plot of the opera, which has brief coherent actions but no overall relationship, and it may be a representation of *zaum* in a musical form.

Pratella's manifesto referred to harnessing the 'musical soul' of machines to use in new compositions. In March 1913, the manifesto, 'The Art of Noises', by the Futurist painter Luigi Russolo, attempted to turn this idea into practice, and it is here where the greatest contribution to music by the Futurists – unordered sound, or noise – was introduced. Although these noises could be found in the real world – the sounds of factories, automobiles, trains, or of thunder, the wind, or a waterfall – Russolo was particularly interested in the artificial production of these sounds through the newly invented 'noise intoners,' or *intonarumori*. These devices consisted of a box with a conical speaker and levers that acted as controls to alter the pitch of each noise. Each device created a specific sound and was given a corresponding name like exploders, cracklers, buzzers, or scrapers. In 1914, Russolo composed *The Awakening of a City* scored only for *intonarumori*, but unfortunately none of the intoners has survived and it is impossible to know what they sounded like or how they reproduced their sounds.[30]

In *Victory Over the Sun*, machine sounds appear on the final page of the manuscript music and on page 22, the last, of the libretto. Unlike the Italian use of *intonarumori* that required special musical notation, the sounds here occur while a fermata holds a rest.[31] Although neither source specifies what kind of machine sounds should be used, they are most likely airplane noises because they occur just before an airplane crashes on stage. The pilot then emerges, unharmed except for some damage to his shoe, and proceeds to sing the Aviator's song made up solely of consonants. As strange as this action may be, it is actually based on a true event. The Futurist poet, Vasili Kamensky, briefly became disillusioned with writing around 1910 and began a new career as a stunt pilot. In 1911, his plane crashed during an airshow in Poland. The crash left Kamensky unharmed, but he immediately gave up flying and resumed writing. In 1913, Kamensky presented lectures about his incident, which became a kind of legend to the whole movement.

Ostinati are another recurring element in this music. Although ostinati had long been a convention of Russian music, and are especially evident in the music of Stravinsky at this time, in the hands of the Futurists they become representations of the cyclical patterns and sounds generated by machines. They are used mostly in the accompaniment to melodramatic sections, although occasionally they appear in songs.

Future Research

Many avenues remain unexplored in the case of the fifteen extant pages of manuscript. First, the observations stated here rely on facsimiles of the music reprinted in a book. Locating and examining the original manuscript would show immediately whether the music existed on single sides of paper or on both sides of a single paper, which would help in determining how much music is missing. Colour variations in the ink, which do not come through in a black and white reproduction, could also show whether markings were made at different times or by different hands, and this could show whether the apparent page numbers described above were made at the time of the copying or on some later date, possibly by an archivist. Writing samples by Maria Ender – letters, forms, official documents, etc. – especially if they traversed a significant time period, could confirm that she in fact copied the manuscript as well as provide a method for dating the copies based on handwriting comparison.

The original manuscript may still exist, and its discovery would also answer these questions. Even if it cannot be found, there is a possibility that the music actually was published in 1915 at the same time as Matiushin's other pieces, *Don Quixot'*, *Autumn Dream*, and the *Guide to Studying Quarter-tones for Violin* by Zhuravl', Matiushin's own publishing company. On the back page of these pieces is an advertisement announcing the publication of the first Futurist opera, *Victory Over the Sun*. It is not clear whether this advertisement refers to a score or only to the libretto, nor is it clear whether the announcement was followed by an actual publication. Adding further intrigue is a gap of ten numbers between the plates of the published works.[32] This gap may mean nothing, or it may suggest the existence of a published score or other unidentified music.

Other connections need to be explored in order to understand fully the context and ramifications of *Victory Over the Sun*. Regardless of whether quarter-tones were intentionally used in the opera or not, the Futurists certainly promoted their use as a novel musical idea in their writings in 1914 following the performance. Several quarter-tone composers emerged in Russia around this time, including Arthur Lourié, Ivan Vyshnegradsky, and Marina Scriabina. Lourié was acquainted with the Futurists and some of his contact is documented in Livshits' memoirs, *The One and a Half-Eyed Archer*. Vyshnegradsky was a student at the St. Petersburg Conservatory at the time of *Victory Over the Sun* and he eventually moved to the West and worked on quarter-tone music with Alois Hába. Scriabina, the daughter of Scriabin, wrote theoretical works on quarter-tones. Whether Matiushin led, followed, or was independent of this movement has yet to be determined. Matiushin attended at least one gathering of quarter-tone composers in 1923 and played an unidentified piece for violin and piano.[33] Giorgiy Rimsky-Korsakov, the nephew of the composer, organised these gatherings, and a regular attendee was Dmitri Shostakovich.[34] Research in Russian cabaret also has not yet been fully explored. Art and literary historians have examined this work for over thirty years to establish its importance to those fields, and it will take some time for musicologists to look at possible avenues that will ultimately put this work in its proper musical context.

Notes

1   A. Kruchenykh and M. Matiushin, *Pobeda nad Solntsem* (St. Petersburg: Sviet' Euy, 1913). Music appears on pages 3, 9, 24.

2   Austellung der Akademie der Künste, *Sieg über die Sonne: Aspekte russischer Kunst zu Beginn des 20 Jahrhunderts* (Berlin: Frölich & Kaufmann, 1983), 73-77. Except for the music found in the libretto, the facsimiles in this book, which were not intended for detailed academic scrutiny, are the source for the music used in this essay. Each sheet of music is in black and white and is less than four inches high and two inches wide and are placed four sheets (two across by two down) per page. Consequently, details about the music such as colour differentiation or whether the music is front to back on the

same sheet or on separate pages are impossible to determine, and parts of the music are very difficult to read.

3   See Juan Allende-Blin, 'Sieg über die Sonne' in *Musik-Konzepte 37/38: Aleksandr Skrjabin und die Skrjabinisten II* (July 1984), 168-182.

4   Whether this other source was the original performance materials or another copy is impossible to determine, but the *terminus ante quem* of the Ender copies show that the existing music is not the original performance materials.

5   Examples include missing or altered accidentals, different pitches in the accompaniment due to miscounted ledger lines below the staff, and a slight change in the text.

6   Heinrich Klotz, ed. and Zentrum für Kunst und Medientechnologie Karlsruhe, *Matjuschin und die Leningrader Avantgarde* (Stuttgart-Munich: Oktogon, 1991), 99.

7   Sophie Lissitzky-Küppers, *El Lissitzky: Life, Letters, Texts*, translated by Helene Aldwinckle and Mary Whittall (London: Thames and Hudson Inc., 1968, 1980), 352.

8   Alla Povelikhina, 'Matyushin's 'Total' Theatre', in *Organica: The Non-Objective World of Natiure in the Russian Avant-Garde of the 20th Century* (Cologne: Galerie Gmurzynska, 1999), 75.

9   See *Den'* Dec. 1, 1913, 6 (in Volume 1); *Peterburgskaia Gazeta,* Dec. 4, 1913, 5; *Peterburgskaia Gazeta,* Dec. 8, 1913, 13; and *Russkie vedomosti,* Dec. 13/26, 1913, 6.

10 Mikhail Matiushin, 'Futurizm v Peterburge', *Futuristy: Pervii zhurnal russkikh futuristov,* Nos. 1-2 (1914), 153-157.

11 Aleksei (Aleksandr) Kruchenykh, *Nash Vikhod* (Moscow: Literaturno-Khudozhectvennoe Agenstvo 'Ra', 1996). In English in Volume 1, "First Futurist Shows in the World".

12 Benedikt Livshits, *The One and a Half-Eyed Archer*, translated, introduced and annotated by John E. Bowlt (Newtonville, MA: Oriental Research Partners, 1977), 160-164. In Volume 1,

13 K. Tomashevsky, 'Vladimir Mayakovsky', *Teatr* 4 (1938), 137-150. English translation by Ewa Bartos and Victoria Nes Kirby in 'Victory Over the Sun', *The Drama Review* 15 (1971), 94-101.

14 Gerald Janecek, *Zaum: The Transrational Poetry of Russian Futurism* (San Diego: San Diego State University Press, 1996), 125.

15 Ibid., 125-126.

16 For a study of Futurist evenings, see Anna Lawton, 'Futurist Manifestos as an Element of Performance', *Canadian-American Slavic Studies* 19 (1985), 473-491.

17 R. W. Flint, trans. and ed., *Marinetti: Selected Writings* (New York: Farrar, Straus, and Giroux, 1971), 116-129. For a complete discussion of Italian Futurist theoretical ideas, see Michael Kirby, *Futurist Performance* (New York: Dutton, 1971).

18   See John E. Bowlt, 'Cabaret in Russia', *Canadian-American Slavic Studies* 19 (1985), 443-463, and Livshits [12], 48, 66, 158ff.

19   Bowlt, 'Cabaret in Russia' [18], 444.

20   Ibid., 444.

21   The possible range is due to the unknown quantities of missing pages in the first act and in the second act following the pages with the numbers. The libretto only shows where songs should have been in the opera; it does not show where speech occurred over music. The libretto also does not give any information as to how the music was laid out in the missing manuscript pages. For example, it is impossible to determine how many pages the missing opening music (the three songs prior to the first accounted song on page 6, 'Bully's Song') contained. Therefore, an estimated range is used.

22   Mikhail Matiushin, 'Futurizm v Peterburge' [10], 155-156.

23   Several secondary sources mention this opera, including Charlotte Douglas, 'Birth of a "Royal Infant": Malevich and "Victory over the Sun" ', in *Art in America* 62 (1974), 50; and Stephanie Barron and Maurice Tuchman, *The Avant-Garde in Russia, 1910–1930: New Perspectives* (Cambridge: The MIT Press, 1980), 208. They indicate that sketches by Malevich survive, but mention very little about the remaining elements.

24   Matiushin, 'Futurizm v Peterburge' [10], 154. While Matiushin associates 'simultaneous movement of four completely independent voices' to the music of Reger and Schoenberg, he could have also chosen J. S. Bach or Palestrina because this describes counterpoint, which had been common in music at least since the Middle Ages.

25   Tomashevsky [13], 97-98.

26   Parts of Matiushin's unpublished autobiography in Klotz [6], 89-91.

27   Peter Deane Roberts, *Modernism in Russian Piano Music: Skriabin, Prokofiev, and Their Russian Contemporaries*, Vol. 1 (Bloomington: Indiana University Press, 1993), 3.

28   Caroline Tisdall and Angelo Bozzolla, *Futurism* (New York: Oxford University Press, 1978), 113.

29   Livshits [12], 173.

30   Tisdall and Bozzolla [28], 114-117.

31   The notation Russolo used for the *intonarumori* consisted of a solid line moving horizontally across a staff with movement up or down either diagonally or in a terraced fashion to indicate a change in pitch. Matiushin's score does not have this kind of notation.

32   The plates for *Autumn Dream, Osenni Son,* are numbered 228 and 229, for the piano and violin parts, respectively. The plate for *Don Quixot'* is 240. The *Guide to Studying Quarter-tones for Violin* has no plate numbers.

33   Klotz [6], 97.

34   Laurel E. Fay, *Shostakovich: A Life* (New York: Oxford University Press, 2000), 19.

THE LEGACY

Long live the Future!

John Milner

'ALL IS WELL THAT BEGINS WELL AND HAS NO END':
THE AFTER-LIFE OF
VICTORY OVER THE SUN

1915

Throughout the latter half of 1913 during the gestation of the opera, Kazimir Malevich was also working on related oil paintings. Just as the opening gesture of the performance had been to display and then destroy images of Mikhail Matiushin, Malevich and Aleksei Kruchenykh, so the related paintings were essentially portraits of Futurists. The catalogue of Tramway V: The First Futurist Exhibition of Paintings, which opened in St. Petersburg on 3 March 1915, dates *Portrait of Matiushin, Composer of the Opera Victory Over the Sun,* to 1913, and attributes the *Englishman in Moscow* and the *Aviator* to the following year. Exhibited in 1915, they served to recall attention to the achievements of the opera. Furthermore, the militarism evident in the swords and sabre of the *Englishman in Moscow* had great relevance as war engulfed Europe.

While the opera announced that 'all is well that begins well and has no end!', in fact it ends with a plane that crashes in a bleak and baffling darkened world. This is perhaps an intimation of war, already in 1913 sparking violence in the Balkans and spreading across Europe with the outbreak of World War I in August 1914. The vision offered by the Futurists in *Victory Over the Sun* was a glimpse of a strange world of old ways decaying and, in its place, Strongmen installing a new regime among flashes of light in the darkness. Performed at a time of collapsing authority in southeast Europe where the Austro-Hungarian and the Ottoman empires met, *Victory Over the Sun* could be seen as a glimpse of tectonic friction between Asia and Europe. There were Turkish enemies in the opera and early costume studies by Malevich emphasise their Eastern clothes and turbans. In the light of this, 'all is well that begins well and has no end' strikes an unconvincing, ironic and mocking tone. It is reminiscent of the tone struck by Burliuk and others in their absurd extension of smart urban clothes to provoke the passers-by in the streets of Moscow and St. Petersburg.

Less than a year after the two-night spectacle of *Victory Over the Sun,* Europe was at war and empires were collapsing. This was a wholly new context within which to consider the opera and the activities of the Futurists. War was a subject that had greatly interested the Futurist poet Khlebnikov. Mixing calculations and poetry, he studied the periodicity of battles between great cultures as eagerly as a geophysicist might study earthquakes. His book, *Battles: A New Teaching About War,*[1] was about exactly this, and so was his little book, *Time is the Measure of the World.*[2] Malevich and Matiushin shared his fascination and were revising *Victory Over the Sun* in a more overtly martial and military format.[3]

In a letter to Matiushin of 27 May 1915, Malevich proposed a curtain presenting a black square. Related drawings show powerful, anonymous male warriors carrying weapons like bazookas and shells (right) inscribed with calculations. (Facing page, 1.)

The set drawing that features Rozanova's initials also has fragments of imagery, including a shell, many calculations like those of Khlebnikov, tiny anonymous and busy figures, and geometric planes that eclipse these complex clusters of symbols and images. There are references to the planet Neptune, the Sun, and space flight. A second drawing has calculations for Mars and the Moon (2). Three small conical craft fly towards a great floating trapezium and associated clusters of rectangles. The spacecraft are drawn with shading to indicate volume, while the great geometric planes that they approach appear as flat surfaces gliding weightlessly. The drawing is inscribed by Malevich as, 'Project. Scene 2/8. Victory over the Sun. Back curtain'.[4]

Geometric planes eclipsing imagery was a feature of several of his paintings during 1914 – 1915, but this drawing is important in a new way. These flying geometric forms are no longer anchored within the densely constructed picture space; on the contrary, they indicate dynamic weightless flight. As the words Mars, Moon and flight are written on the drawing, this is clearly interplanetary space in which the great trapezium represents some new kind of object, a flying surface without volume, engines or weight.

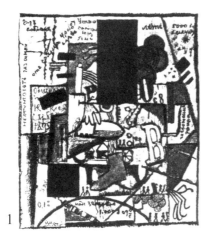

1

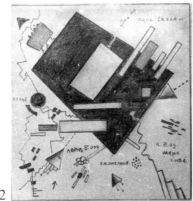

2

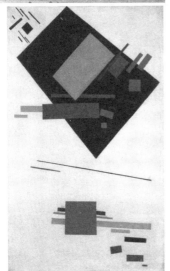

3

The same trapezium plane appears in a painting called *Suprematism* (below, 3, Stedelijk Museum, Amsterdam).[5] Together, this drawing for a backdrop in a new war-torn version of *Victory Over the Sun*, and the painting *Suprematism*, show plainly the relationship of Kruchenykh and Matiushin's opera to the new mode of painting that Malevich launched at The Last Futurist Exhibition of Paintings: '0,10' (Zero-Ten) displayed in Petrograd (formerly St. Petersburg) from 17 December 1915 to 17 January 1916. This painting, *Suprematism*, hung below the *Black Square* of Malevich. Both of these paintings are directly associated with designs for the unrealised 1915 production of *Victory Over the Sun.* Other paintings in the exhibition may relate directly to the opera. One of them, for example, is titled *Flight of an Airplane* (Stedelijk Museum, Amsterdam).

Suprematism became immensely influential. An immediate transition to Suprematism can be traced in the 1916 designs made by Olga Rozanova, first to illustrate Kruchenykh's book *War*,[6] and then in her collage illustrations for Kruchenykh's *Universal War*.[7]

Below left:
K. Malevich, *Suprematism*, 1915, Stedelijk Museum, Amsterdam

1920

A radically changed environment again confronted Futurism when the disastrous war led to revolution in Russia in 1917. Yet the opera *Victory Over the Sun* flickered into life in the collective, public and politicized culture of the new Communist regime. Malevich was directly involved in the design of this production along with the painter Vera Ermolaeva, who in 1919 invited Malevich to teach at Vitebsk. As a result, Vitebsk became a centre of Suprematist experiment where the concepts of Malevich were explored in new directions and communicated to a younger generation.

 Here Ermolaeva encouraged the involvement of the newly founded Suprematist collective UNOVIS (Affirmers of the New Art) to work out and realise the project for the modest production of *Victory Over the Sun* performed there on 6 February 1920. Designs were illustrated in the *Unovis Almanac*, No. 1, published that year.

Malevich and Ermolaeva designed the costumes for the Futurian Strongman (previous page, below left and right, respectively).[8] The set design by Ermolaeva for the second act survives in a linocut print (facing page, above), in which two robotic Futurist figures stand confident and proud in front of the Futurist House in the final scene. Her design reiterates the motif of a dense mass of forms swelling forwards and outwards, towards the spectators, like an immense effusion of energy used by Malevich in his design of 1913. Ermolaeva's version is made up of strongly modelled cylindrical and cubic forms held back by circular and rectangular planes and another curved plane. The robotic future-men adopt a lively pose in front of this great powerhouse, and there is a suggestion of music in the central structure, that still remotely recalls a guitar.

It is not clear if this evokes an acceptable image of the new Communist society, but it was certainly collectively produced and made public. The ideological requirement was not easy to avoid. In addition, utopian visions of ideal society in art, literature, architecture and planning were frequent in 1920. Any suggestion in the original opera that a victory over the sun might lead to darkness policed by Futurian Strongmen would have lost its ironic quality in this context, when even science fiction addressed the sociological aims of the new society. The anarchic Futurists had to switch on the optimistic rhetoric of ideological commitment, shown here in the energy that these confident, faceless and identical robots display.

1923

Among the most creative people in the UNOVIS group was Lazar (El) Lissitzky. He developed the idea of a puppet version of the opera. Since 1913 an element of the automaton was evident in *Victory Over the Sun*. Communal work in collectives, the imagery of the masses, and of the powerful anonymous worker gave new significance to these designs under the Communist ideology. Lissitzky's puppets were never realised as a theatrical event, but the figures and costumes, now greatly refined and

elegantly resolved by Lissitzky, were published as a portfolio of colour lithographs in 1923.[9] The outer cover of the portfolio featured a single letter, 'F' for 'Figurinen' ('Figures'), and Kruchenykh is shown holding it in a photograph of the early 1920s, overleaf. It literally exemplifies the Futurists' *The Letter as Such*, about which Lissitzky had learned a great deal, not least from Malevich.

    The title sheet (below) of Lissitzky's portfolio announces: 'All is well that begins well and has no end'. Lissitzky does this, not in *zaum* language, but by mixing European languages to declare that 'Alles ist bien was good nachinaetsia et hat no finita'. Lissitzky unites nations, including the workers of the world. From the first page Lissitzky's concept of *Victory Over the Sun* is politicized. It has a more explicit ideology than any earlier version.

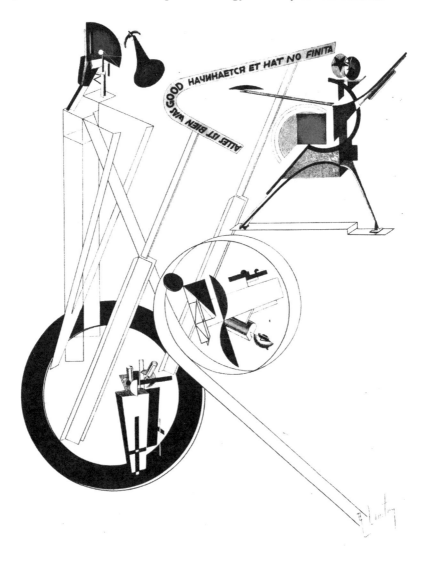

The same sheet introduces four major protagonists from the action of the opera. From a high platform the Radio-speaker, clad in a red shirt, tips his loudspeaker to make his announcement to the masses. Far below in a dark circle the funeral attendants stand gloomily by, coffin-shaped in black and white, top hats polished into shining cylinders, retaining crosses that have, as far as possible, been de-Christianized. The Traveller Through All Centuries[10] whirls past in a loop, scarcely touching the globe, as he races through time and space, perched behind the spinning propeller of his skeletal flying machine. Here, too, are the sloping Cowards anxiously looking over their shoulders in the strange new world, and a Guard, with peep-hole eye and a lock for a mouth, a Bully who is all spikes, and an Old-Resident smiling at the past. The resilient Sportsmen are more at home in the new world, and above it all the New Man strides confidently forward with his arms and legs outstretched, a new version of Leonardo da Vinci's universal man, though now displaying, for all to see, the red square at his heart and the red star in his head. This dynamic and anonymous figure is Soviet universal man.

Lissitzky's characterization is convincingly achieved with wit, lightness of touch, and technical precision. The characters can easily be paired with those of Malevich, though they are brought up to date, transformed and politicized. What has made this possible, strangely enough, is Lissitzky's knowledge of Suprematism, learnt from this later stage of Malevich's work. Lissitzky's forms implied that his figures could be constructed. The feet of the New Man can be built with materials, though in fact Lissitzky often made his structures ambiguous or spatially contradictory. In his introduction to the portfolio Lissitzky acknowledged the opera's phonetic poetry as the basis of his designs. He also points out that each colour signifies a material for construction, so that yellow might be soft copper and black be tarnished iron.

When Lissitzky explained that modern man has the Sun torn down from the sky, he implicitly spoke of the old authority, of autocratic rule, now overthrown by revolution. As his dynamic New Man shows, Lissitzky did not promote a gloomy view of the new order. He seemed convinced that Communism could make a New Man fit for the new era.

The internationalism in this message characterizes Lissitzky's approach. At the time of publication he was liaising between Russia and Germany, establishing cultural links between the Bolsheviks and activist art groups in Western Europe including Dada, De Stijl, and the Bauhaus.

Lissitzky's was the last version of *Victory Over the Sun* made by creative people still connected to the original performances of 1913. The world had swept from urban capitalism, through world war, revolution, and into a socialist ideology promoting itself abroad. It is remarkable that *Victory Over the Sun* had the means and the meaning to adapt each time. The Traveller Through All Centuries was still on the move.

1980, 1983, 1984, 1989, 1993, 1999, 2009 …

The Time-Traveller is still moving. More productions have followed since World War II. Its creators are dead, but their opera of two nights is still revived, dusted down and performed. It made its first run of three nights at the Los Angeles County Museum on 5 – 7 September 1980, and later at the Hirshhorn Museum in Washington D. C., and in Tokyo. It appeared at the Brooklyn Academy of Music in New York in November 1983, at Toulouse in March 1984, and at Munich in April-May that year. It reappeared in Russia in 1989 at Leningrad and Moscow, in Vienna and Moscow in 1993, and in a menacing performance at the Barbican Theatre, London, in 1999.

As his creators intended, the Traveller Through All Centuries is still globetrotting through time, proclaiming his message with confidence that 'all is well that begins well and has no end.'

Notes

1   V. Khlebnikov, *Battles 1915 – 1917: A New Teaching About War* (Petrograd: Zhuravl / The Crane, 1914). He predicted the end of a great state in 1917.

2   V. Khlebnikov, *Vremya Mera Mira / Time is the Measure of the World* (Petrograd: Zhuravl / The Crane, 1916).

3   At this time Matiushin was working on a projected opera called *War*. This may have been a related or even the same project.

4   See Susan P. Compton, *The Worldbackwards: Russian Futurist Books 1912 – 1916* (London: The British Library, 1978), 111; Charlotte Douglas, *Malevich* (London: Thames and Hudson, 1994), 82; and John Milner, *Kazimir Malevich and the Art of Geometry* (New Haven and London: Yale University Press, 1996).

5   The painting is now in the Stedelijk Museum in Amsterdam.

6   A. E. Kruchenykh, *Voyna* (*War*), engravings by Olga Rozanova (Petrograd: Andrei Shemshurin, 1916), 16 leaves, 100 copies.

7   A. E. Kruchenykh, *Vselenskaya Voyna* (*Universal War*) (Petrograd: Andrei Shemshurin, 1916), 14 pages, 12 collage illustrations by Olga Rozanova.

8   Dzhon E. Boult [John E. Bowlt] *Khudozhniki Russkogo Teatra 1880 – 1930*.

Katalog-Rezone. Stat'i. Knyaz' N. D. Lobanov-Rostovsky ob istorii kollektsii (Moscow: Isskustvo, 1994), 140-41.

9   El Lissitzky, *Figurinen. Die plastische Gestaltung der Elektro-Mechanischen Schau 'Sieg uber die Sonne'* (Hannover: Leunis and Chapman, 1923). See Boult (Bowlt), *Khudozhniki Russkogo Teatra* [8], 187 ff. Lissitzky had hoped to publish the portfolio of lithographs in Russian in 1920 – 21. The German edition included ten figure designs.

10   He is called the Globetrotter through Time in the German translation.

BIBLIOGRAPHY
Press Reviews are found in Volume 1

Allende-Blin, Juan. 'Sieg über die Sonne. Kritische Anmerkungen zur Musik Matjuiins'. *Musikkonzepte*, Volume 37/38: 'Alexander Skrjabin und die Skrjabinisten II'. Edited by Heinz Klaus Metzger and Rainer Riehn. Munich, 1982/84.

Andreoli-di-Villers, Jean-Pierre. *Le Premier Manifeste du Futurisme: Édition Critique avec, en Facsimilé, le Manuscrit Original de F. T. Marinetti*. Ottawa: Éditions de l'Université d'Ottawa, 1986.

Artaud, Antonin. *Selected Writings*. Edited by Susan Sontag. Berkeley: University of California Press, 1988.

Artaud, Antonin. *Theater and its Double.* New York, 1958.

Austellung der Akademie der Kunste. *Sieg über die Sonne: Aspekte russischer Kunst zu Beginn des 20 Jahrhunderts*. Berlin: Frölich & Kaufmann, 1983.

Baedeker, Karl. *Baedeker's Russia 1914*. Newton Abbot: David & Charles, 1971.

Bakhtin, M. M. *Estetika sloveskogo tvorchestva.* Moscow, 1979.

Barron, Stephanie and Maurice Tuchman, Editors. *The Avant-Garde in Russia, 1910 – 1930: New Perspectives*. Cambridge, MA: The MIT Press, 1980.

Bartlett, Rosamund. *Wagner and Russia.* Cambridge: Cambridge University Press, 1995.

Bartos, Ewa and Victoria Nes Kirby. 'Victory Over the Sun'. *The Drama Review*, Vol. 15, No. 4, Autumn 1971, 107-124. First English translation of *Victory Over the Sun*, plus memoirs and press reviews.

Basner, Elena. ' "It is We Who Are Blind; They See the New Sun". Futurism and the Futurists in the Mirror of the Russian Press of the 1910s'. *Russian Futurism*. State Russian Museum. St. Petersburg: Palace Editions, 2000.

Bauermeister, Christiane and Nele Hertling, Editors. *Sieg über die Sonne. Aspekte russischer Kunst zu Beginn des 20. Jahrhunderts*. Berlin: Fröhlich & Kaufmann, 1983.

Bazarov, K. 'Diaghilev and the Radical Years of Modern Art'. *Art and Artists*, Vol. 10, No. 4, July 1975, 6-15.

Beaujour, Elizabeth. 'Zaum'. *Dada/Surrealism* 2, 1972, 13-18.

Blanchot, Maurice. 'Reflections on Nihilism: Crossing the Line'. *Friedrich Nietzsche.* Edited by Harold Bloom. New York: Chelsea House Publishers, 1987.

Bobrinskaia, E. 'Motivs "preodoleniia cheloveka" v estetike russkikh futuristov'. *Voprosy iskusstvovedeniia* 1, 1994, 199-212.

Bonnefoy, Claude. *Conversations with Eugene Ionesco.* New York: Holt, Rinehart and Winston, 1970.

Boult, Dzhon E. [John E. Bowlt]. *Khudozhniki Russkogo Teatra 1880 – 1930. Katalog-Rezone. Stat'i. Knyaz' N. D. Lobanov-Rostovsky ob istorii kollektsii.* Moscow: Isskustvo, 1994.

Bowlt, John E. 'Cabaret in Russia'. *Canadian-American Slavic Studies* 19, 1985, 443-463.

Bowlt, John E. 'Natalia Goncharova and Futurist Theatre'. *Art Journal*, Vol. 49, No. 1, Spring 1990, 44-51.

Bowlt, John E. 'The Spirits of Music'. *The Isms of Art in Russia 1907 – 30.* Cologne: Galerie Gmurzynska, 1977.

Bowlt, John E. "The 'Union of Youth'". *Russian Modernism: Culture and the Avant-Garde, 1900 – 1930.* Edited by G. Gibian and H. W. Tjalsma. Ithaca: Cornell University Press, 1976, 165-187.

Bowlt, John E. 'Vom Symbolismus zum suprematismus'. *Vom Klang der Bilder. Die Musik in der Kunst des 20. Jahrhunderts.* Karin v. Maur, Editor. Munich: Prestel, 1994.

Clark, Katrina. *Petersburg, Crucible of Revolution.* Cambridge, Mass: The MIT Press, 1995.

Compton, Susan P. *The World Backwards. Russian Futurist Books 1912 – 1916.* London: The British Library, 1978.

Dadswell, Sarah. Unpublished doctoral thesis: 'The Spectacle of Russian Futurism: The Emergence and Development of Russian Futurist Performance, 1910 – 1914'. University of Sheffield, 2005.

Douglas, Charlotte. 'Birth of a "Royal Infant": Malevich and *Victory Over the Sun'*. *Art in America*, 62, 1974.

Douglas, Charlotte. *Swans From Other Worlds: Kasimir Malevich and the Origins of Abstraction in Russia.* Ann Arbor: UMI Research Press, 1976.

Enukidze, N. 'Pobeda nad solncem najavu' / 'The Real Meaning of Victory Over the Sun'. *Iskusstvo avangarda: yazyk mirovogo obsceniya.* Ufa, 1993, 81-89.

Erbslöh, Gisela. *Pobeda nad Sontsem': Ein futuristisches Drama von A. Kruchenykh.* Munich: Verlag Otto Sagner, 1976.

Esslin, Martin. *The Theater of the Absurd.* New York: Vintage Books, 2001.

Evreinov, Nikolai. *Teatr kak takovoi.* St. Petersburg: Sovremennoe iskusstva, 1912. 2nd edition Berlin, 1923.

Fauchereau, Serge. *Malevich.* Translated by Alan Swan. New York: Rizzoli International Publications, Inc., 1993.

Faye, Laurel E. *Shostakovich: A Life.* New York: Oxford University Press, 2000.

Flint, R. W., Translator and Editor. *Marinetti: Selected Writings.* New York: Farrar, Straus, and Giroux, 1971.

Gadamer, Hans-Georg. *Truth and Method.* New York, 1975.

Galerie Gmurzynska. *Organica: The Non-Objective World of Nature in the Russian Avant-Garde of the 20th Century.* Cologne: Galerie Gmurzynska, 1999.

Gleizes, Albert and Jean Metzinger. *Du "Cubism".* Paris: Ed. Eugène Figuière, 1912. Translated into Russian as *O "Kubizm"* by Ekaterina Nizen. St. Petersburg, 1913.

Gojowy, Detlef. *Arthur Lourié und der russische Futurismus.* Regensburg: Laaber, 1993.

Gojowy, Detlef. 'Musikalische Ideen des russichen Futurismus'. *Glossarium der Avantgarde.* Edited by Aleksandar Flaker. Graz: Droschl, 1989.

Gourianova, Nina. *The Russian Futurists and Their Books*, Editor. Translated by Andrew Bromfield. Collection of facsimiles of A. Kruchenykh and V. Khlebnikov, *Worldbackwards*; Kruchenykh, *Hermits*; Kruchenykh, *Half-Alive*; Kruchenykh, *Explodity!;* Kruchenykh, Khlebnikov, *A Game in Hell*; Khlebnikov, *Selected Poems.* Moscow: Avant-Garde, and Paris: La Hune, Libraire Editeur, 1993.

Graver, Lawrence and Raymond Federman, Editors. *Samuel Beckett: The Critical Heritage.* London: Routledge, 1979.

Gray, Camilla. *The Russian Experiment in Art, 1863 – 1922.* Revised by Marian Burleigh-Motley. New York: Thames and Hudson, Inc., 1986.

Howard, Jeremy. *The Union of Youth . An Artists' Society of the Russian Avant-Garde.* Manchester: Manchester University Press, 1992.

Janecek, Gerald. 'A *Zaum*' Classification'. *Canadian-American Slavic Studies* 20, 1986, 37-54.

Janecek, Gerald. *Zaum: The Transrational Poetry of Russian Futurism.* San Diego: San Diego State University Press, 1996.

Kämper, Dietrich, Editor. *Der musikalische Futurismus.* Regensburg: Laaber-Verlag, 1999.

Kandinsky, Vasily. 'On the Question of Form'. *The Blaue Reiter Almanac* (1912), Edited by Wassily Kandinsky and Franz Marc. English translation edited by Klaus Lankheit. London: Thames and Hudson, 1974.

Khardzhiev, Nikolai. 'Is materialov o Maiakovskom'. *30 dnei*, No. 7, 1939, 82-85.

Khardzhiev, N. I. 'Polemchnoe imy'. *Pamir* 2, 1987.

Khlebnikov, Velimir. *Collected Works of Velimir Khlebnikov*, Vol. 1 *Letters and Theoretical Writings.* Translated by Paul Schmidt. Edited by Charlotte Douglas. Cambridge, Mass: Harvard University Press, 1987.

Khlebnikov, Velimir. *The King of Time. Selected Writings of the Russian Futurian.* Translated by Paul Schmidt. Edited by Charlotte Douglas. Cambridge, Mass: Harvard University Press, 1985.

Kirby, Michael. *Futurist Performance.* New York: Dutton, 1971.

Klotz, Heinrich, Editor, and Zentrum für Kunst und Medientechnologie Karlsruhe. *Matjuschin und die Leningrader Avantgarde.* Stuttgart: Oktogon, 1991.

Kruchenykh, Aleksei. 'New Ways of the Word' / 'Novy puti slova', in *The Three / Troe.* St. Petersburg: Zhuravl', 1913. Translated into English in this volume, and by Anna Lawton and Herbert Eagle in *Russian Futurism Through Its Manifestoes, 1912 – 1928.* Edited by Anna Lawton. Ithaca: Cornell University Press, 1988.

Kruchenykh, Aleksei. *Nash Vykhod.* Edited by Vasily Rakitin and Andrei Sarabianov. Moscow: RA, 1995.

Kruchenykh, Aleksei. *Our Arrival [Nash Vykhod]. From the History of Russian Futurism.* Edited by Vasily Rakitin and Andrei Sarabianov. Translated by Alan Myers. Moscow: RA, 1995.

Kruchenykh, Aleksei. *Pamiat' teper' mnogoe razvorachivaet: Iz literaturnogo naslediia Kruchenykh.* Edited by Nina Gurianova. Berkeley: Berkeley Slavic Specialities, 1999.

Kruchenykh, Aleksei. *Pobeda nad solntsem.* St. Petersburg: EUY, 1913.

Kruchenykh, Aleksei*, Pobeda nad Sontsem: Ein futuristisches Drama von A. Kruchenykh.* Translated by Gisela Erbslöh. Munich: Verlag Otto Sagner, 1976.

Kruchenykh, Aleksei. *Victoire sur le Soleil.* Translated by V. and J.-C. Marcadé, with notes and afterword. Lausanne: L'Age d'Homme, 1976.

Kruchenykh, Aleksei. *Victory Over the Sun.* Translated by Ewa Bartos and Victoria Nes Kirby in *The Drama Review*, Vol. 15, No. 4, Autumn 1971. First English translation.

Kruchenykh, Aleksei. *Vosropshem [Let's Grumble].* St. Petersburg: EUY, 1913.

Kruchenykh, Aleksei. *Vzorval [Explodity].* St. Petersburg: EUY, 1913.

Kruchenykh, A. and V. Khlebnikov. *Slovo kak takovoe [The Word as Such].* St. Petersburg: EUY, 1913.

Larionov, Mikhail and Ilya Zdanevich. 'Pochemu my raskrashivaemsia: Manifest futuristov'. *Argus*, Christmas 1913.

Law, Alma H. 'Vittoria sul sole: note sugli allestimenti del 1913 e 1920'. *Polifonia: da Malevi a Tat'jana Bruni 1910 – 1930*, Exhibition catalogue. Milan: Electa, 1998.

Lawton, Anna. 'Futurist Manifestos as an Element of Performance'. *Canadian-American Slavic Studies* 19, 1985, 473-491.

Lawton, Anna and Herbert Eagle, Editors and translation. *Russian Futurism Through its Manifestoes, 1912 – 1928*. Ithaca, NY: Cornell University Press, 1988.

Leach, Robert. 'A Good Beginning: "Victory over the Sun" and "Vladimir Mayakovsky, a Tragedy" Reassessed'. *Russian Literature* 13, 1983, 101-116.

Lissitzky, El. *Figurinen / Puppets. Victory Over the Sun.* 10 Lithographs. Hanover, 1923.

Lissitzky-Küppers, Sophie. *El Lissitzky: Life, Letters, Texts.* Translated by Helene Aldwinckle and Mary Whittall. New York: Thames and Hudson, Inc., 1980.

Livshits, Benedikt. *Polutoraglazy strelets* (1933) and New York: Chekhov Publishing Corporation, 1978.

Livshits, Benedikt. *The One and a Half-Eyed Archer* (1933). Translated into English by John E. Bowlt. Newtonville: Oriental Research Partners, 1977.

Lourié, Arthur Vincent. 'K′ muzyke vysscgo chromtizma'. *Strelets*, No. 1, St. Petersburg, 1915. Re-published by Detlef Gojowy. *Neue sowjettische Musik der 20er Jahre.* Regensburg: Laaber-Verlag, 1980.

Magebrov, A. S. *Zhizn v teatre (A Life in the Theatre)*, Vol. 2. Leningrad: Academia, 1932, 272-285.

Maiakovskii, Vladimir V. *Polnoe sobranie sochinenii*, 13 vols. Moscow: Khudozhestvennaia literatura, 1955 – 1959.

Majakowski, Wladimir. *Vladimir Majakowski Tragödie.* Facsimile reprint of *Vladimir Mayakovsky: A Tragedy*, with drawings by David and Vladimir Burliuk. Berlin: Friedenauer Presse, 1985.

Malevich, K. S. *Essays on Art – Vol. 1 1915 – 1933.* London: Rapp & Whiting, 1969.

Marcadé, Jean-Claude. 'Post-Face. La Victoire sur le Soleil, ou le merveilleux futuriste comme nouvelle sensibilité'. *La Victoire sur le soleil: Opéra.* Lausanne: L'Age d'homme, 1976, 65-97.

Marcadé, Valentine. *Le Renouveau de l'art pictural russe.* Lausanne: L'Age d'Homme, 1971.

Marinetti, F. T. 'Declaration of Futurism'. Facsimile of his own English translation in Jean-Pierre Andreoli-de-Villers. *Le Premier Manifeste du Futurisme: Edition Critique avec, en Facsimilé, le Manuscript original de F. T. Marinetti*. Ottawa: Editions de l'Université d'Ottawa, 1986.

Marinetti, F. T. *Il teatro di varietà*. Milan: Direzione del movimento futurista, 1913.

Marinetti, F. T. *Uccidiamo il chiaro di luna*. Milan: Edizione Futuriste di Poesie, 1911.

Markov, Vladimir. *Russian Futurism: A History*. Berkeley: University of California Press, 1968, and London: Macgibbon & Kee, 1969.

Matiushin, Mikhail. 'Futurizm v Peterburge'/'Futurism in St. Petersburg', *Futuristy. Pervyi zhurnal russkikh futuristov / Futurists: First Journal of Russian Futurists*, No. 1-2, Moscow, 1914, 153-157. Translated by E. Bartos and V. Nes Kirby in *The Drama Review*, Vol. 15, No. 4, 1971, and in Volume 2 of this collection.

Matiushin, Mikhail. 'The Memoirs of Mikhail Matiushin'. *Experiment*, Vol. 1, 1995. Edited by John E. Bowlt. Institute of Modern Russian Culture, Los Angeles: Charles Schlacks, Jr., Publisher, 211-233.

Matiushin, Mikhail. 'On the Book by Gleizes and Metzinger *Du Cubisme*'. *Union of Youth* 3, St. Petersburg, March 1913. Translated into English by Linda Dalrymple Henderson in *The Fourth Dimension and Non-Euclidean Geometry in Modern Art*. Princeton: Princeton University Press, 1983, 368-375.

Matiushin, Mikhail. 'Russkii kubofuturizm: Otryvok iz neizdannoi knigi', *Tvorcheskii put' khudozhnika'. Nashe nasledie* 2, 1989.

Matiushin, M. V. 'Tvorcheskii put' khudozhnika', IRLI, fond 656, p. 79, cited in Konstantin Rudnitsky, *Russian and Soviet Theatre: Tradition and the Avant-Garde*. London: Thames and Hudson, 2000.

Matjuschin, Michail. 'Meine Musikalische Kompositionen 1932/34'. *Matjuschin und die leningrader Avantgarde*. Edited by Heinrich Klotz. Stuttgart: Oktogon, 1991.

Matjusin, Michail. 'Russkie kubo-futuristy'. *K istorii russkogo avangarda / The Russian Avant-Garde*. Edited by Nikolaj Chardziev. Stockholm: Hylaea Prints, 129-187.

Maur, Karin v., Editor. *Vom Klang der Bilder. Die Musik in der Kunst des 20. Jahrhunderts*. Munich: Prestel, 1994.

Mayakovsky, Vladimir. 'Theater, Cinema, and Futurism' (1913). Translated by Helen Segall in *Russian Literature Triquarterly*, Ardis, 1975, 181-183. Originally published in *Kine-zhurnal*, No. 14, Moscow, 27 July 1913, 24-25.

Milner, John. *Kazimir Malevich and the Art of Geometry*. New Haven and London: Yale University Press, 1996.

Misler, Nicoletta. 'Il Colore del spazio'. *Polifonia: da Malevic a Tat'jana Bruni 1910 – 1930*. Exhibition catalogue. Milan: Electa, 1998.

Nakov, Andréi. *Kazimir Malewicz, le peintre absolu*, Vol. 1. Paris: Thalia Editions, 2007, 287-334.

National Gallery of Art, Washington D. C. *Kazimir Malevich*. Exhibition catalogue, 1990.

Nikitaev, Aleksandr. 'Obieruty i futuristicheskaia traditsiia'. *Teatr*, 11, 1991, 3-7.

Ouspensky, P. D. *Tertium Organum, The Third Canon of Thought, A Key to the Enigmas of the World*. Translated by Nicholas Bessaraboff and Claude Bragdon. London: Routledge & Kegan Paul, 1923 and 1981. First published St. Petersburg, 1911.

Parnack, V. *Gontcharowa. Larionow: L'art Décoratif Théâtral Moderne*. Paris: Edition 'La Cible', 1919.

Parton, Anthony. *Mikhail Larionov and the Russian Avant-Garde*. Princeton: Princeton University Press, 1993.

Petrova, Yevgenia, Editor. *The Russian Avant-Garde: Representation and Interpretation*. State Russian Museum. St. Petersburg: Palace Editions, 2001.

Petrova, Yevgenia. *Russian Futurism*. State Russian Museum. St. Petersburg: Palace Editions, 2000.

Petrovskaia, I. *Teatr i zritel' rossiiskikh stolits 1895 – 1917*. Leningrad, 1990.

Povelikhina, Alla. 'Matyushin's "Total" Theater'. *Organica: The Non-Objective World of Nature in the Russian Avant-Garde of the 20th Century*. Cologne: Galerie Gmurzynska, 1999.

Powelichina, Alla. 'Michail Matjuschin – Die Welt als organisches Ganzes'. *Matjuschin und die leningrader Avantgarde*. Edited by Heinrich Klotz. Stuttgart: Oktagon: 1991.

Powelichina, Alla. 'Über die Musik im Schaffen des Malers Michail Matjuschin'. *Sieg über die Sonne*. Edited by Christiane Bauermeister and Nele Hertling. Berlin: Fröhlich & Kaufmann, 1983.

Richter, Hans. *El Lissitzky. Sieg über die Sonne. Zur Kunst des Konstruktivismus*. Cologne, 1958.

Roberts, Peter Deane. *Modernism in Russian Piano Music: Skriabin, Prokofiev, and their Russian Contemporaries*, 2 vols. Bloomington: Indiana University Press, 1993.

Rosenfild, Alla, Editor. *Defining Russian Graphic Arts 1898 – 1934: From*

Diaghilev to Stalin. Piscataway: Rutgers University Press and The Jane Voorhees Zimmerli Art Museum, 1999.

Rowell, Margit and Deborah Wye. *The Russian Avant-Garde Book 1910 – 1934.* New York: The Museum of Modern Art & Harry N. Abrams Inc., 2002.

Rudnitsky, Konstantin. *Russian and Soviet Theatre: Tradition and the Avant-Garde.* London: Thames and Hudson, 2000.

Sarabjanov, Dimitri. 'Malevic tra cubismo francese e futurismo italiano'. *Polifonia: da Malevic a Tat'jana Bruni 1910 – 1930. Bozzetti teatrali dell'avanguardi russa.* Exhibition catalogue. Milan: Electa, 1998.

Scholle, Christine. 'Futurisches Theater. Majakovskij – Krucenych – Chlebnikov'. *Zeitschrift für Ästhetik und allgemeine Kunstwissenschaft,* 27, 1982.

Scholle, Christine. 'Krutschonykh – Sieg über die Sonne'. *Das russisches Drama.* Edited by Bodo Zelinsky. Düsseldorf: Bagel, 1986, 239-251.

Sharp, Jane A. 'The Russian Avant-Garde and Its Audience: Moscow, 1913', *Modernism / Modernity: Politics/Gender/Judgement,* Vol. 6, No. 3, 1999, 91-116.

Shklovsky, Viktor. 'On Poetry and Trans-Sense Language'. Translated and annotated by G. Janecek and P. Mayer. *October* 34, 1985, 3-24.

Slonim, M. *Russian Theatre from the Empire to the Soviets.* London: Methuen, 1963.

Stedelijk Museum Amsterdam. *Kazimir Malevich.* Exhibition catalogue, 1989.

Sukhoparov, S. *Sud'ba budetlianina.* Munich, 1992.

Tarkka, Minna. 'Reconstructing Victory Over the Sun', *Malevich,* Special Issue of *Art & Design,* Vol. 5, No. 5/6, London, 1989, 76-80.

Terёchina, V. N. and A. P. Zimenkov, Editors. *Russkii Futurism. Teoria. Praktika. Kritika. Vospominanija.* Moscow: Nauchnoe Izdanie, 1995. Contains Mikhail Matiushin, 'Futurism v Peterburge. Spektakli 2,3,4, i 5-go dekabrja 1913'.

Terras, Victor. *A History of Russian Literature.* New Haven: Yale University Press, 1991.

Tillberg, Margareta. *Coloured Universe and the Russian Avant-Garde. Matiushin on Colour Vision in Stalin's Russia 1932.* Stockholm: Stockholm University, 2003.

Tisdall, Caroline and Angelo Bozzolla. *Futurism.* New York and London: Thames and Hudson, 1977, 1985.

Tomashevsky, K. 'Vladimir Mayakovsky'. *Teatre,* No. 4, 1938, 138-150. Cited in E. Bartos and V Nes Kirby, 'Victory Over the Sun' in *The*

Drama Review, Vol. 15, No. 4, 1971, 120, and in *Sieg über die Sonne,* edited by Christiane Bauermeister and Nele Hertling. Berlin: Fröhlich & Kaufmann, 1983, 86-87.

Veis, Zoia and Viacheslav Grechnev. 'Tragediia "Vladimir Mayakovsky"'. *S Maiakovskim Po Sankt-Peterburgu.* St. Petersburg: Izdanie nauchno-populiarnoe, 1993.

Volkov, Nikolai. *Meyerkhold.* Moscow-Leningrad, 1929.

Wagner, Richard. 'Art and Revolution'. *Die Kunst und die Revolution*, 1849, Vol. III, 8-41; 'The Art Work of the Future'. *Das kunstwerk der Zukunft*, 1849, Vol. I, 194-206; and 'Opera and Drama'. *Oper und Drama*, 1852, Vol. III, 222-320 & Vol. IV, 1-229. All volumes of *Sämtliche Schriften und Dichtungen.* Leipzig: Breitkopf & Härtel, 1912 – 1914.

Zdanevich, Ilya. *Mnogovaia poeziia.* Manuscript (1914). Archive of the State Russian Museum, St. Petersburg, f.177, doc. 22.

Zelinsky, Bodo, Editor. *Das russisches Drama.* Düsseldorf: Bagel, 1986.

Zhakkar, Zh.-F. *Daniil Kharms i konets russkogo avangarda.* St. Petersburg, 1995.

INDEX TO VOLUMES 1 AND 2

Entries to Volume 1 are preceded by 1/, followed by page numbers. Where entries are found in Volume 2 only they are indicated by page numbers alone. If they follow entries to Volume 1 the page numbers are preceded by 2/.

Absurd 40, 43n22, 70, 74

Airplane, Aviation 1/140; 2/38, 70, 80

Allegory 20

Alogism 10, 31, 33, 36, 39, 40, 41
    theatre of 31-44
    visual arts 10, 33; *see*
        Malevich, Kazimir

Anarchy 17, 35

Anti-modernist 20

Anti-utopia 35

Apocalypse 17

Apprehension 79

Argonauts 37

Artaud, Antonin 32-33, 38, 39
    theatre of cruelty 40

Artists' Society 'Union of Youth'
    see Union of Youth

Bakst, Lev 22, 104

Balla, Giacomo 9, 92

Ballets Russes 22, 97

Balmont, Konstantin 1/33, 38-39

Bartlett, Rosamund 20, 21

Bat, The 36, 37, 105

Beyonsense 32, 35; *see*
    Transrational, Zaum

Blanchot, Maurice 35

Blok, Aleksandr 1/126; 2/24, 30n17, 37, 38, 62
    *The Puppet Booth /
    Balaganchik* 1/126; 2/24-26, 37

Bolshakov, Konstantin 27

Books, Russian Futurist 1/12, 15, 16-17, 38; 2/85-88

Bowlt, John E. 19

Breton, André 44n26

Briusov, Valerie 53, 62

Brullov, Karl 1/38

Burliuk, David 1/14. 15. 21, 34, 102, 131, 136; 2/9, 38, 58, 86, 88, 95, 96, 104, 120

Cabaret 36, 105-106, 113

Cannons / *pushki* 1/35, 36, 37

Carroll, Lewis 1/10

Chaos 1/22; 2/10-11, 34, 40, 41

Church 17

Compton, Susan 19, 21, 23

Consciousness 78-79

Consonants 1/140, 154n16, 156n26; 2/51, 59, 63, 65n13, 79

Content 18, 37, 54

Craig, Edward Gordon 25, 89

Create, to 41, 54

Crooked Mirror, The 24, 36, 37, 105; *see* Evreinov, Nikolai

Cube, of the stage 69, 76

Cubism/ist 1/122; 2/9, 13, 18, 50, 69-70, 75, 87, 91, 97n2

Cubo-Futurism 10, 87, 90, 97n2

Curtain 1/35; 2/29, 30n33

Dada 35
    Zurich 33

Dawn 1/154n15
Dehumanization 40, 44n23
Diaghliev, Sergei 20, 22, 28, 97,
    98n12
Dimension 1/122; 2/53, 55, 77
    fourth 50, 53, 71, 77-78
    multi- 93
    third, three 1/128; 2/71, 74, 77
    two 53, 71
Direction See Space
Disharmony 40
Displacement 1/121; 2/35, 70
Dissonance 1/140; 2/33, 35, 36,
    39, 40, 52, 54, 59, 111
Dostoevsky, Fedor 48, 51, 57
Dramatis Personae 1/29-32, 130
    Attentive Workman 1/32, 39,
        90, 91, 92, 93; 2/62, 73
    Aviator 1/32, 39, 96, 97, 98,
        99, 140; 2/37, 38, 39, 62,
        79, 80, 92, 93, 94, 95,
        109-110, 112
    Bully 1/30, 58, 59, 60, 61, 62,
        63; 2/61, 64, 89, 125
    Certain Person with Bad
        Intentions 1/30, 56, 57, 58,
        59, 62, 63, 66, 67; 2/32, 61,
        62, 90
    Chorus 1/30, 37, 66, 67, 68, 69,
        78, 79; 2/90
    Cowards 1/31, 39, 84, 85, 140;
        2/61, 91, 125
    Enemies in Turkish costumes
        1/30, 66, 67, 89; 2/91
    Enemy 1/30, 62, 63; 2/90
    Fat Man 1/32, 34, 35, 39, 86, 87
        90, 91, 92, 93; 2/17, 40, 61-62
        73, 74, 75, 76, 79, 91, 92
    Frightened One
        See Young Man

    Funerarians 1/30, 36, 74, 75;
        2/61, 90
    Mottled Eye 1/31, 84, 85,
        154n17; 2/61
    Nero and Caligula 1/9, 29, 36,
        52, 53, 54, 55; 2/60, 62, 73,
        89, 93
    New 1/31, 84, 85; 2/61, 62, 79
    New Man 124-125
    Old Resident 1/32, 90, 91;
        2/62, 92, 125
    One and Many 1/31, 38, 78, 79,
        80, 81; 2/76
    Reader 1/31, 84, 85; 2/32, 37,
        61, 62, 79, 91
    Sportsmen 1/30, 66, 67, 94, 95,
        96, 97; 2/61, 62, 90, 92
    Strongmen 1/29, 34, 35, 36, 39,
        50, 51, 52, 53, 66, 67, 68, 69,
        70, 71, 98, 99, 124, 140;
        2/18, 39, 60, 61, 62, 72, 78,
        89, 91, 92, 109
    Sun Carriers 1/31, 36, 78, 79;
        2/91
    Talker on a Telephone 1/30, 37,
        78, 79; 2/61
    Traveller Through All Centuries
        1/29, 34, 35, 52, 53, 54,
        55, 56, 57, 58, 59; 2/37,
        38, 60-61, 62, 87, 89, 92,
        124-126
    Young Man 1/32, 33, 38-39,
        92, 93, 94, 95; 2/32, 65n13
Dust 1/34-35; 2/74
Dynamism 9, 10

Early Morning / Ranee Utro
    1/120; 2/88, 91, 93, 94, 96
Eclipse 1/38; 2/71-72, 78-80, 90,
    91, 93, 96

Ender, Maria 1/103-118; 2/102ff,
    112
Ermolaeva, Vera 122-123
Evreinov, Nikolai 19, 21, 24, 26,
    28, 32, 36, 37, 38, 105
    total theatre 36, 37, 38
    theatre as such 41
Exter, Alexandra 97
Eye 90-91, 93, 94

Filonov, Pavel 1/22, 23, 24, 137;
    2/88
First All Russian Congress of
Futurian Bards 1/14-15, 122; 2/86
First Futurist Exhibition of
    Paintings Tramway V 119
First Futurist Theatre in the World
    1/18, 19, 20, 21, 130, 131; 2/31
Flagellants 1/129 and note; 2/32,
    49
Folk theatre See Theatre
    traditions 20
Form 1/129; 2/18, 37, 54
Fort, Paul 22
Freud, Sigmund 32
Futur teatr 1/18, 19; 2/95
Future, the 71, 72
Futurism/ists 1/122
    Italian 9, 17, 19, 33, 38, 54, 57,
        63, 92, 94, 97n2, 105, 106,
        110-111
    Russian 1/121, 126, 137, 138,
        139; 2/9-11, 17, 18, 19, 33,
        34, 38, 41, 42, 57, 58, 60, 62,
        63, 85, 86, 91, 92, 95, 104,
        106, 111

Gadamer, Hans Jorg 41
Game 34
Genesis 17

Geometry 79
    Euclidean 77
    non-Euclidean 77
Gesamtkunstwerk 21ff
    See Total Work of Art
Gleizes, Albert and Jean
Metzinger, On "Cubism" 69, 75
Goncharova, Natalia 9, 13, 19,
    22, 26-27, 28, 85, 87
Gorodetsky, Sergei 33
Gravity 38
Guro, Elena 1/15, 16; 2/12, 51, 52,
    59, 103, 104, 108, 112
    Autumn Dream / Osenii Son
        108, 112
    Barrel Organ / Sharmanka 51,
        108, 112
    Don Quixote / Don Quixot'
        108, 112

Harlequin 38
Howard, Jeremy 14, 25
Hylaea 14, 58

Incorrect 50-53, 59-60
Infinity 35
Innovation 35
Intuitive 41
Ionesco, Eugene 33
Iron age 1/36-37; 2/34, 80
Irony 41
Irrational 10, 53, 77, 78

'Jabberwocky' 1/10
Jarry, Alfred 32

Kamensky, Vasily 38, 87, 90-91,
    94-95, 112
Kandinsky, Vasily 20, 21, 22, 23,
    35

Kharms, Daniil 33
Khlebnikov, Viktor/Velimir 1/7
    8, 16, 28, 33, 40, 44-47
    (Prologue), 121, 127 129, 142;
    2/7, 9, 11, 18, 31, 41, 45, 52, 59,
    60, 69, 70, 71, 72, 73-74, 75,
    79-80, 85, 86, 94, 95, 96, 101,
    120
    *Battles: A New Teaching About
        War* 120
    *Time is the Measure of the
        World* 120
    'War – Death' 52, 59
Khlysty 1/129 and note; 2/32
Kliun, Ivan 91, 96
Komissarzhevskaya, Vera 21, 22,
    24, 28
Kruchenykh, Aleksei 1/12, 13,
    14-15, 16, 22-25, 28, 33, 34,
    35, 37, 39, 50-99, 121, 122,
    125, 130; 2/7, 10, 11, 18, 19,
    20, 21, 23, 28, 31-44, 69, 70,
    72, 73, 74, 78, 81, 85, 86, 88,
    89, 91, 92, 94, 95, 101, 103,
    104, 119, 121, 123-124
    Bridge, The / Most 31, 33, 37
    *Declaration of the Word as
        Such* 58-59
    Explodity / Vzorval 59-60, 85,
        87
    'First Futurist Shows in the
        World' 1/130-144
    Gly-Gly 31, 33
    Let's Grumble / Vozropshchem
        31, 37, 41, 51, 59, 85
    'New Ways of the Word' 37,
        47-55, 59-60, 62-63, 70
    Our Arrival 80
    The Poetry of Mayakovsky 92
    Pomade / Pomada 58

Universal War 121
Victory Over the Sun:
    Libretto 1/50-99
    Commentary on 1/8-9,
        33-49, 123, 124, 125, 127,
        130-133, 140-143; 2/11,
        18-20, 23, 28, 36, 37, 39, 40,
        41, 42, 60-64, 69-81
War 121
Word as Such, The 62, 86
Kulbin, Nikolai 1/126; 2/19, 86,
    105

Language 32-34, 47-56
    Universal 59; *see*
    Transrational, Zaum
Larionov, Mikhail 13, 19, 26-27,
    28, 85, 87; *see* Rayism
Last Futurist Exhibition of
    Paintings 0.10 121
Le-Dantu, Mikhail 1/141
Light 18
Lissitzky, El 102-103, 123-126
    Figures / Figuren 123-126
Livshits, Benedikt 1/125-129;
    2/9, 18, 20, 86, 89, 90, 93,
    103-104, 110, 113
Lotev, Anton 27
Lourié, Arthur 110, 113
Lubok (folk prints) 25, 85
Lugné-Poe 22
Luna Park 1/18, 19, 20, 21, 26;
    2/22, 36, 90

Magebrov, A. S.
    Life in the Theatre 1/41, 135,
        141-142, 144n7
Malevich, Kazimir 1/12, 13, 14-15,
    16-17, 22-25, 28, 33, 34, 37, 38;
    2/7, 9, 10, 11, 13, 14, 18, 21, 23,

28, 29, 34, 35, 41, 42, 69, 74, 75,
    81, 85-98, 101, 104, 119, 120-123
Book illustration 1/16-17;
    2/85-87
Interview 1/22, 141; 2/11, 34
Aviator 33, 38, 95
Black Square 1/38; 2/121
Cow and Violin 33
Englishman in Moscow 33, 96,
    119
Flight of an Airplane 121
Knifegrinder 9, 87
Portrait of Matiushin 119
Suprematism 121
Union of Youth 7 87, 97n2
Mansion House Scenes 25-26
Marinetti, Filippo T. 17, 19, 34, 105
Markov, Vladimir (Woldemar
    Matvejs) 1/156n25; 2/13, 14
Matiushin, Mikhail 1/12, 13, 14-15,
    22-25, 28, 33, 121, 122, 125,
    130; 2/7, 11, 12, 18, 21, 23, 28,
    34, 42, 69, 70, 81, 85, 86, 88,
    89, 94, 95, 99, 101-115, 119, 120
Compositions:
    Autumn Dream / *Osenii Son*
        108, 112
    Barrel Organ / *Sharmanka*
        108, 112
    Don Quixote / *Don Quixot'*
        108, 112
    Harlekin 108
*Guide to Studying Quarter-
    tones for Violin* 110ff
Interview 1/22, 141; 2/11, 34
Review: 'Futurism in St.
    Petersburg' 1/121-124; 2/69-
    70, 107, 108
Music 81, 99, 101-115; see
    Victory Over the Sun: Music

and Score
Mayakovsky, Vladimir 9, 41, 92
    *Vladimir Mayakovsky: A
        Tragedy* 1/20, 21, 22, 121,
        123, 124, 125-127, 130-131,
        132-140, 141, 144n1; 2/13,
        21, 36, 86, 88, 101, 104
Meyerkhold, Vselvolod 19, 21,
    22, 24, 26, 28, 31, 35-37
Mimetics 23
Mind, the 10, 69, 78, 79, 81
Modern life 50, 70, 72
Modernism/ist 20, 23, 25
Modernity 48, 54, 57, 80
    myth of 35
Moon 1/38; 2/17, 34, 73, 76, 91
Moscow Art Theatre 23, 25, 37
Movement 9-11, 50
Music 70, 99
Music hall 19
Myth 80

Narrative(s) 19, 22
Nature 17
Naturalism 23, 24
Neologism 1/7-8, 150-152, 153-156;
    2/51, 52, 57, 59, 63, 64, 72,
    79-80; *see* 'Jabberwocky', and
    Kruchenykh, A., 'New Ways of
    the Word'
New Man 125
Nihilism 35, 39
Nothingness 35

Odoevsky, Prince Vasily 1/34, 36
Old Believers 1/39; 2/32
Opera 20
Ouspensky, P. D.
    Tertium Organum 48, 77-78,
        79, 81

Parody 20, 24, 35, 36-39
Past, the 71, 72
Perception 9-10, 50, 70, 79
Perspective
   box 93
   inverse 27, 28
   reverse 74
Philistine 41
Phonics 39, 40
Picasso, Pablo 92, 96
Pierrot 38
Pink Lantern 27-28
Planets 17
Play 40ff
   as such 41
Poet as shaman 72, 80
Popular traditions 20
Pratella, Francesco Balilla
   'Technical Manifesto of Futurist
     Music' 110-111
Presence 40-41
Prutkov, Koz'ma 36
Pushkin, Alexander 1/33-40;
   2/48, 54, 57
Psychological
   drama 25
   method 23
Psychologism 38
Quarter tones 18, 23, 70, 99, 102,
   108-110, 113

Rational 10, 11, 41, 53, 57, 73,
   75, 76
Rayism 87-88
Reger 1/121; 2/99, 108
Renaissance, Italian 17
Revelation 35
Revelation, Book of 17
Revolution 17, 20
Riddle 34

Rozanova, Olga 1/18, 19, 131;
   2/9, 13, 85, 86, 95, 96, 120, 121
Rupture 17
Russolo, Luigi
   'The Art of Noises' 111-112

Schoenberg, Arnold 1/121;
   2/99, 108
Scriabin, Alexander 21, 22, 23
Sensation 9, 10, 48, 79
Severini, Gino 9
Shamanism 1/129n1; 2/71, 72, 80
Shchukin, Sergei 69
Shift (*sdvig*) 18
Shiftology 1/8
Shiskov, Varlaam 1/129 and
   note; 2/49; *see* Flagellants, Old
   Believers
Shkolnik, Josif 1/22, 23, 127,
   137; 2/13, 14, 88
Silver Age 38
Slap in the Face of Public Taste, A
   48, 57, 58, 62
Slavism 70, 72, 79-80
Space 71, 73, 74-78, 94
   Dimensions of *See* Dimension
   Directions of 74-78, 94
Space-time 11, 71, 72, 74, 76-78,
   94
Speaking in tongues 32
Stage
   as a box 69ff, 81, 93
   modernist 28
Stanislavsky, Konstantin 23, 24, 37
Stereometry 1/128-129; 2/93
Stravinsky, Igor 22, 92, 112
Stray Dog, The 36, 37, 105, 106
Sun 1/22, 34, 36, 37, 38, 141;
   2/17, 34, 62, 70, 71, 72, 73, 76,
   79, 90, 91, 93-94, 96, 124; *see*

Pushkin

Suprematism 33, 35, 101, 122, 125

Supremus 33

Surrealism 35, 44n26

Symbolism/ists 1/38; 2/20, 21, 22, 24, 37, 38, 50-51, 53, 55, 62-63

Synaesthesia 23-25

Tairov, Alexander 97

Target 51

Tatlin, Vladimir 96
    Tsar Maksemian and his Disobedient Son Adolf 25, 88

Teatr Futu 26-28

Theatre
    absurd 33
    of alogism 31-44
    avant-garde 25
    as such 36, 37, 41
    of cruelty 40
    experimental 32
    folk 18-20, 25
    Futurist 26-28, 101, 105
    of illustration 23
    modern/ist 24, 26, 27, 28
    naturalist 23-25, 27, 28
    of parody 36
    public 36
    rayist 27
    realism 23, 26
    surrealist 33
    total 36, 37, 38, 105
    transformation of 28
    transrational 33
    variety 36

Thought 48-49

The Three / *Troe* 1/12, 16-17, 130; 2/23, 47-55, 70, 86-87, 91, 94, 95, 108

Time 10, 11, 15, 17, 25, 38, 71, 72, 73-78, 94

Time-body 77-78

Tolstoy, Leon 48, 57

Tomachevsky, K. 104, 109-110

Transformation 20

Transrational 10, 18, 34, 57, 77, 78, 86; *see* Beyonsense, Zaum

Transverse 1/34

Trap for Judges, A 51, 52, 59, 95

Udaltsova, Nadezhda 9

Udder 1/38; 2/76

Union of Youth 1/123, 125, 130, 131, 139, 143; 2/12-14, 25, 26, 86, 88, 104, 107

Universe 92

UNOVIS / Utverditeli NOVogo ISkusstovo / Affirmers of the New Art 122-123

Utopia/ism 35

Uusikirkko 1/12, 13, 14-15, 130; 2/85-86, 104

Veil *See* Curtain

Victory 35, 38, 71, 72

Victory Over the Sun
    as Anti-bourgeois 28
    Audience reaction 1/41, 124, 127, 140, 141-142
    Backdrops, Costumes and Staging 1/29-32, 41, 120, 123, 124, 128-129, 130, 131, 140, 141-142; 2/18, 67, 69ff, 83, 89-98, 120-123
    Backdrops illustrated 1/49, 65, 73, 77, 83, Commentary on 10, 74, 75, 76, 89-94, 96-97
    Costumes
        Illustrated 1/29-32, 60

Commentary on
  41, 88, 89, 90, 91
Dramatis Personae *See*
  Costumes, Dramatis
  Personae
and Folk theatre 19-20, 105-106
Interview 1/22,141; 2/34
Later productions 119-127
Libretto, the 1/50-99; *see*
  Kruchenykh, Aleksei
Lighting 1/128, 140; 2/18,
  87-88, 90, 91, 93
its Meaning 1/141
Music and Score 1/48, 61, 100,
  103-118, 121, 124. 125, 131,
  141; 2/18, 23, 99, 101-115;
  see Matiushin, Mikhail
Opening scenes 1/41, 127, 140,
  141-142; 2/20, 29, 89, 96-97;
  see Livshits, Benedikt,
  Magebrov, A. S.
as an Opera 1/15, 131;
  2/105-106
on the Performance 1/123-124,
  127-129, 140, 141-142; 2/64
Performers 1/123, 125, 140, 143
Plot 1/22, 141; 2/60-62
as Political satire 98n13
as Politicized 123-125
as Popular theatre 28
Posters 1/18-21, 131-133; 2/85,
  95; *see* Rozanova, Olga
Press Reactions 1/121, 122,
  142-143, 145-149
Prologue 1/7-8, 44-47, 127,
  140, 143; 2/60, 70, 72, 79-80,
  81, 89
as Public theatre 36, 101

Rehearsals 1/123; 2/103-104,
  107
Reviews 1/120, 121-124, 125,
  128-129, 138-140, 142-143
as Revolutionary 28-29, 94
as Space-time *See* Space-time
as a Spectacle 1/130
and Technology 1/140
Tenth land 1/39, 78, 79, 84-99,
  154n13; 2/61, 62, 74, 75, 76,
  80
as Theatre of alogism 31-44
Translation, on the 1/7-9
Vladimir Mayakovsky: A Tragedy
  See Mayakovsky, Vladimir
Void 1/38
Volcano 1/38
Vowels 1/140, 154n16; 2/51, 59,
  63, 65n13

Wagner, Richard 20ff, 29
War 34, 35, 120
Weight 54
Weightlessness 39, 40
Word, the 45, 47-65, 70, 72, 79-80
Word as Such, The 86
Worldbackwards 52, 74 (as
  World in Reverse), 98n13

Zaum 1/8-9, 129, 153n8, 154n16,
  155n24; 2/10, 18, 23, 28, 32,
  39, 42n8, 57-65, 75, 86, 87, 95,
  111, 12; *see* Beyonsense,
  Transrational
Zaum Realism 86, 97n2
Zdanevich, Ilya 1/141; 2/32, 33
Zheverzheev, Levky Ivanovich
  1/125, 143; 2/13-14, 88, 89, 90